Choosing and using
Climbing Plants

Choosing and using
Climbing Plants

Barbara Abbs

NEW HOLLAND

This paperback edition published in 2008 by
New Holland Publishers (UK) Ltd
London • Cape Town • Sydney • Auckland

Garfield House
86–88 Edgware Road
London
W2 2EA
United Kingdom
www.newhollandpublishers.com

80 McKenzie Street
Cape Town 8001
South Africa

Unit 1, 66 Gibbes Street
Chatswood, NSW 2067
Australia

218 Lake Road
Northcote, Auckland
New Zealand

ISBN 978 1 84537 973 5

Senior Editor: Clare Hubbard
Editor: Jo Smith
Design: Peter Crump
Illustration: Coral Mula
Production: Hazel Kirkman
Editorial Direction: Rosemary Wilkinson

5 7 9 10 8 6 4

Reproduction by Pica Digital Pte Ltd, Singapore
Printed and bound in Malaysia by Times Offset (M) Sdn Bhd

NOTE
The author and publishers have made every effort to ensure
that all instructions given in this book are safe and accurate,
but they cannot accept liability for any resulting injury or loss
or damage to either property or person, whether direct or
consequential and howsoever arising.

Page 2: Boston Ivy, *Parthenocissus tricuspidata*, in glorious
autumn colour.

Opposite: It can take a number of years before a wisteria
produces its elegant clusters of scented, lilac blooms.

INVASIVE PLANTS

The following climbing plants mentioned in this book
have become serious problems when introduced into
certain areas. Check with your nurseryman before
introducing non-native climbers, particularly in warm,
fertile regions.

Akebia quinata
Ampelopsis brevipedunculata
Anredera cordifolia
Cardiospermum grandiflorum
C. halicacabum
Euonymus fortunei
Ipomoea indica
Lonicera japonica
Lonicera periclymenum
Macfadyena unguis-cati
Passiflora spp.
Pueraria montana lobata
Thunbergia alata
T. grandiflora
Wisteria sinensis

GARDEN SAFETY TIPS

* When pruning it is advisable to wear eye protection
and gardening gloves. If pruning large hedges and
trees take great care when working overhead or from
a ladder; it is best to call in a professional.

* When appylying fertilizers and weedkillers always
follow the manufacturer's instructions, wear gloves
and wash your hands after use. Store safely in clearly
labelled containers.

* Keep all tools and equipment clean and dry and
store safely.

Contents

Introduction

ROSES, HONEYSUCKLE, CLEMATIS AND WISTERIA are the names which immediately spring to mind when climbing plants are mentioned. Ivy, Virginia creeper and sweet peas are the other popular climbing plants that everyone has heard of, but most of us would be hard pushed to name any more. However, there are many other wonderful climbers that are less well known and that deserve close examination. Some are suitable for "problem" gardens and difficult places and all can be used in a variety of ways. Unlike shrubs and perennials which stay where you have planted them, all sorts of exciting things happen with climbers because they are constantly on the move.

Garden designers spend a small fortune on buying large trees to give instant height and maturity to a garden. Height in a garden, either from trees, surrounding walls, or from mounds and banks, gives a sense of scale and security. These features add an intermediate level between earth and sky. In some places, like prairie gardens or seaside gardens, the designer may want to create a feeling of being very small and insignificant in nature, but most of us prefer to feel enclosed and in proportion with our surroundings. For those who are impatient and lacking a small fortune, there is another way to create seclusion, increase interest and add height to a garden – by using climbers.

Climbers are especially useful when creating a garden because most grow very quickly. A barren patch can be transformed in a season or two without enormous expense. Because the majority are fast growing, you can use climbing plants as permanent features or just as a temporary measure while shrubs and hedges are growing. Climbers are versatile, too. Not only do they grow up, but they also hang down. Some can be trained into "standards", like wisteria and ivy, while others will happily crawl over the ground, disguising unsightly objects and festooning shrubs.

HOW CLIMBERS CLIMB

Climbers are fascinating plants and they do not all climb in the same way. How they attach themselves to their supports affects how they can be used in the garden. There are four main types:

• Woody twiners are often referred to as lianes and are common in tropical forests. The long stems looping from tree to tree are familiar to film-goers as the ropes that Tarzan swings from. Wisteria is the best-known woody twiner, common in gardens. Twiners have twining stems which twist round a support, either clockwise or anti-clockwise.

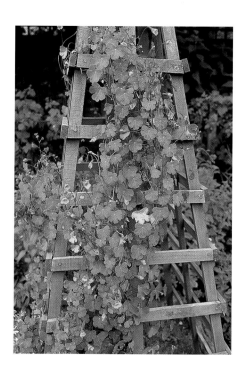

Left: The flowers and picturesque twining trunk of a mature *Wisteria sinensis* show up beautifully against the white paint and fresh green trim of this cottage.

Right: *Tropaeolum tuberosum* var. *lineamaculatum* 'Ken Aslet' makes a fine focal point, scrambling up an obelisk made of pleasantly weathered timber.

• Tendril climbers support themselves by means of flexible tendrils which will twist round and hold on to anything they come across. They can have leaf stem tendrils where the stalks of the leaves twist round any likely support (for example, nasturtiums and clematis); stem tendrils, such as grapes and marrows; or tendrils derived from leaves, like the sweet pea and the Chilean glory flower (*Eccremocarpus scaber*). The tendrils of Virginia creeper (*Parthenocissus quinquefolia*) have tiny adhesive pads at their ends.

• Other climbers have adhesive adventitious roots which develop from the stems. These include ivy, climbing hydrangeas (*Hydrangea anomala ssp. petiolaris*) and *Campsis radicans*. Others have aerial roots, including the cheese plant (*Monstera deliciosa*) and the philodendrons.

• The last group of climbers include the roses (ramblers, climbing and pillar roses), which hoist themselves through trees, shrubs or manmade structures using their thorns to hold on with. The tropical climber, the cat's claw vine (*Macfadyena unguis-cati*), has tendrils equipped with incredibly fine hooks which can penetrate the tiniest of cracks in brick and stone walls.

Then there is another group of plants, the scramblers, which are grown in the same way as climbers. These produce long, bendy stems which grow up through a neighbouring shrub, then side branches which grow out sideways to stop the main stem from slipping down again. Blackberries and the winter jasmine, *Jasminum nudiflorum* are good examples.

ABOUT THIS BOOK

This book is a practical guide to choosing and using climbers. It begins with details of how to plant, train, support and care for your climbers, followed by a useful section on selecting climbing plants for different soils and situations. If you plan to erect a pergola on the north side of your house and you have acid soil, for example, the plants you grow will be different from those chosen to clothe a pergola in full sun and in chalky soil. You may long for a glamorous wisteria, but if the conditions are not suitable, a flourishing climber of more modest appearance is preferable to a starved-looking wisteria with few or no flowers. You have to accept the limitations of your plot and work with them and this is as true for climbers as for every other plant.

The book goes on to more aesthetic issues, with chapters on using climbers for colour and designing with climbers. There are suggestions on how to make your garden appear larger by using certain colours, or how to choose climbers to create a romantic atmosphere. You will also find advice on using climbers in difficult places and for particular design problems, such as screening and creating focal points. The Classic Combinations chapter suggests ways to combine two or more climbing plants to complement and enhance each other to give you double the pleasure.

Even vegetable gardeners and indoor gardeners can find places for climbing plants. A shady corner in a vegetable garden can grow runner beans or gourds successfully and a hot conservatory can be shaded by using climbers that will thrive under the glass to create a leafy canopy.

The book ends with a directory of climbing plants, arranged alphabetically for easy reference. Here you will find details of many of the fascinating plants mentioned throughout the book. Welcome to the world of the varied and versatile climbing plant.

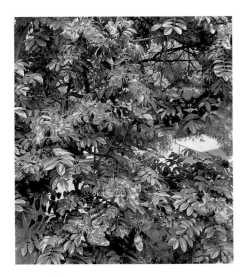

Campsis radicans, the Trumpet vine, is a self-clinging climber, that will happily attach itself to walls or trees.

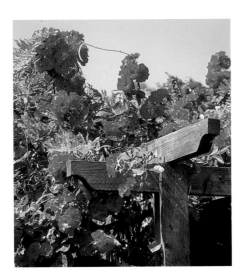

Roses, like this climber *R.* 'Meihati' 'Sparkling Scarlet' are shown to advantage on a pergola. In a tree, the thorns would hook on, but on a pergola it needs tying in.

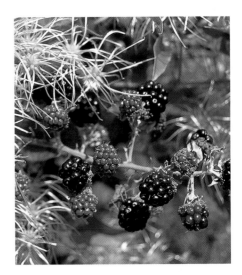

A wild blackberry, a scrambler which uses prickles to cling to a host plant, grows with *Clematis vitalba*, Old Man's Beard, to make an unplanned but perfect autumn partnership.

CHOOSING AND CARING FOR CLIMBERS

*H*owever you want to use climbers, whether it is to screen, to veil, to draw attention to an object or to frame a view, the plants need to be suited to the soil, climate and aspect and require some care after planting. There is no need to be unduly worried about caring for climbers, they require no more or less care than any other type of plant in the garden that you wish to flourish for a number of years. Selecting the right plant is essential. There are climbers for different soils, for sun or shade and for different climates and positions. For example, honeysuckles are easy to please with regard to soil and temperature but are prey to aphids on hot walls, while clematis need their roots shaded, and most roses flower better in full sun.

The delicate yellow flowers of *Rosa banksiae* 'Lutea' and the bright pink of the thornless rose 'Zephirine Drouhin', together with the wall shrub, vivid blue *Ceanothus* 'Cascade' make an eye-catching mid-summer picture.

Preparation and planting

EARLY AUTUMN IS A GOOD TIME TO PLANT HARDY CLIMBERS as the weather is generally mild and moist. However, if you are planting container-grown plants, you can plant at any time of year, provided the ground is not frozen. Bear in mind that if you plant in summer and the weather is dry, you must be prepared to water thoroughly every day using a 9-litre (2-gallon) can of water. Tender climbers, such as passion flowers, are best planted in late spring/early summer, when the soil has warmed up. Before you begin to dig the soil, soak the plants well. The addition of seaweed concentrate to the water will help the roots to establish quickly.

GARDEN KNOW-HOW

Preparing the ground for planting

Soil preparation is vital to get climbing plants off to a good start. The soil beneath a wall can be very dry and often quite alkaline as a result of lime leaching from the mortar. If you plan to grow any lime-hating plants, it is worth doing a soil test.

1 Unless the soil has already been dug over or is well cultivated, dig a hole about 1m (1yd) square and two spits, or spade's depths, deep. Add a good quantity of organic matter, such as well-rotted farmyard manure, leafmould or garden compost (A) plus two handfuls of bonemeal to the soil (B). If the soil is clay, add some lime to the subsoil (C). For very heavy clay, add peat, grit or sand to open up the texture and mix it in well (D).

2 On very dry ground, soak the soil in the hole well (E), then line the hole with lawn mowings, up-ended turfs (F), vegetable peelings or other material from the compost heap. If you make your own compost and are not sure whether all the annual weed seeds have been killed, bury the compost at the bottom of the hole.

3 In chalk and sandy soils, add broken-up rotted turfs and extra bulky manures. Chalk soil will need liberal mulches added each year. If the ground is badly drained, line the hole with clinker (G), brushwood, polystyrene or even fibreglass.

PLANTING

The planting holes in the prepared soil need to be about 30 x 30cm (12 x 12in) for most container-grown climbers and 45 x 45cm (18 x 18in) for climbing roses. Put in any necessary stakes or supports when the hole has been dug. In very dry weather, fill the hole with water and let it drain away. Plant the plant to the same depth as it was in the container. Spread the roots out in the hole and cover with soil. Back-fill the hole almost to the top, leaving a slight hollow round the plant to help watering. Firm well in and then soak again thoroughly with water.

After planting, mulch the area with chipped bark, gravel or dry soil to retain moisture around the plant's roots. You will need to keep the climber well watered during the first season unless it is very wet or your soil is exceptionally retentive. One way of ensuring that enough water is carried directly to the roots of the plant is to insert a length of plastic pipe into the soil before you begin planting.

In the winter, after any frost, check that the plant roots have not lifted out of the ground. If they have, firm them in again.

GARDEN KNOW-HOW

Planting against a wall

Walls generally offer sheltered conditions for climbing plants and will help slightly tender plants to survive outside. However, the aspect of the wall will make a big difference to the conditions it offers. Study your site carefully to determine how warm or sheltered the conditions are and how much light it offers and choose your plants to suit.

Take care choosing plants for walls which get early morning sun. During cold weather when a frosty night is followed by a bright sunny morning, frozen flower buds can be damaged as they thaw too fast. For this reason, choose plants that come into flower after the last expected frosts, such as roses or late-flowering clematis including *Clematis* 'Duchess of Albany, 'Ernest Markham' or 'Hagley Hybrid'.

Do not dig the hole too near the wall – plant climbing roses and other vigorous woody climbers at least 45cm (18in) away and guide the stems of the plant towards the wall with sturdy canes. Passion-flowers (*Passiflora*), however, can be planted at 20cm (8in) from the wall as they enjoy the dry conditions there.

1 Insert the stake firmly into the soil at the bottom of the hole. Keep the stake at an angle, leaning towards the wall, to guide the plant in the right direction (A).

2 Replace some of the prepared soil and firm it in well before you put in the plant so that it will be at the correct depth which is the same as it was in its container or in the nursery (B).

3 Spread the roots out in a fan-shape away from the wall. Any roots that are damaged should be cut off cleanly (C). Fill the hole, firming it but leaving a slight depression to help with watering (D).

Training climbers

ALL CLIMBING PLANTS NEED SUPPORT, whether it is a tree or hedge, wall or trellis, pergola or wigwam. For annual or short-lived climbers, a temporary support is adequate, such as a wigwam of bean canes or a lightweight trellis. For perennial climbers, any wooden support should be sturdy and treated with a preservative. The poles should be set firmly in the ground, either in concrete or in metal post spikes as the structure will need to last for many years and the plant may well become very heavy. Walls should be pointed and in good condition. Some vigorous climbers, especially self-clingers like ivy or climbing hydrangea, may damage walls if they have loose or crumbly mortar.

PRACTICAL PROJECT

Training plants on walls

Securing wires to a wall or fence is one of the easiest ways of providing support for climbing plants that need it.

1 Hammer vine eyes into the wall. They need to be spaced about 2m (6ft) apart and each row should be 50–60cm (20–24in) apart.

2 Thread strong galvanized wire through one vine eye and, using pliers, fix it in position by bending about 15cm (6in) of its length back on itself and twisting together. Take the wire through each vine eye until the whole length is complete. Allow another 15cm (6in) and then cut the wire. Pull the wire tightly, bend it back on itself around the last vine eye and twist together (A).

3 Attach the plant stems to the wires using plant ties, raffia or soft string. Do not tie the stems too tightly (B).

TRAINING SELF-CLINGING CLIMBERS

Even self-clinging climbers, such as climbing hydrangea (*Hydrangea anomala ssp. petiolaris*) and ivy, take a little time to support themselves so fixing them to the wall, fence or pergola helps them to get established. As these fixings do not need to be long lasting, use plant hooks that are glued to the wall or a plant tie stapled to a fence – these should last in place long enough for the aerial roots of the plants to take over. Do not use U-shaped staples directly over the plant stems as they will soon restrict the stems' growth. Instead use the staples to fix plant ties or horizontal wires to the support and then carefully tie the plant stems in place.

WALL SHRUBS AND WOODY CLIMBERS

Wall shrubs tend to lean away from the wall, so some support is beneficial. Likewise, woody climbers such as roses need strong and permanent support to guide them in the right direction. A good choice are flat or eyelet vine eyes embedded in the wall, through which wires are threaded. Good quality trellis is another excellent option for roses and woody climbers.

Fixing trellis to a wall

Attaching trellis to wooden battens fixed to the wall allows for air circulation behind the trellis. If the wall is painted and needs regular maintenance, use hooks or hinges to attach the trellis to the fixed battens, so that the trellis panels can be carefully folded down along with the plants while repairs are made.

1 Measure the trellis panel and work out where the top and bottom cross-pieces of the trellis will go on the wall. Mark the place in pencil.

2 Cut two battens of 5 x 2.5cm (2 x 1in) timber to the same width as the trellis panel. Drill holes in the battens at 45cm (18in) intervals. Holding the battens against the lines marked on the wall, mark the positions of the holes (A).

3 Drill holes in the wall and fix the battens into place with screws and wall plugs (B).

4 Attach the bottom of the trellis panel to the bottom batten with a hinge fixing (C) and secure the top of the trellis to the top batten with hooks or a bolt fixing.

5 Finally, attach the plant stems to the trellis using plant ties or soft string (D).

TWINING CLIMBERS

Some twining climbers will happily weave their own way through trellis but many, such as scramblers, will need attaching to it. Do not attach the stems too tightly and use a soft material. Wire can damage the plant stems, particularly with soft-stemmed climbers like clematis. Raffia or jute twine are good. Plastic adjustable ties and plant rings are easy to use but may be obtrusive. Strips of old nylon tights are ideal – flexible, soft, long-lasting and usually an unobtrusive beige. Tie them neatly and trim loose ends.

For the curling leaf stems of clematis and other tendril climbers, a finer mesh needs to be added to the trellis. Different grades of plastic mesh are readily available and a 5cm (2in) mesh is ideal. Simply fix it to the front of the trellis with staples.

Pruning climbers

THERE ARE TWO MAIN REASONS FOR PRUNING. The first is to keep the plant in the place you want and to the size you want; the second is to improve the amount and display of flowers and leaves. Not all climbing plants need pruning: a vigorous climbing rose like 'Rambling Rector' or *R. brunonii* can be left to grow through a tree indefinitely, as can *Clematis montana* or Virginia creeper (*Parthenocissus quinquefolia*). However, in most gardens climbing plants do need to be kept within bounds and they flower better and at a lower level if regularly pruned.

How and when to prune

• **Plants that flower before midsummer on stems that have developed the previous year** Prune immediately after flowering. Prune about one third from each stem that has flowered, making a slanting cut just above a node (A).

• **Climbers that flower on new stems produced the same year** Prune in late winter or early spring before buds develop. Thin the stems if necessary, removing complete stems from near the base of the plant and cut out any dead wood. Cut the stems of very vigorous climbers back by about two-thirds to keep them within their allotted space (B).

• **Evergreen climbers that are grown for their flowers** Prune immediately after flowering, cutting back to healthy buds (C).

• **Other evergreens** Prune in spring when there is no longer a danger of frost. Cut back dead or damaged branches to healthy wood and remove any other growth that is necessary to keep the plant shapely and in its allotted space. Established ivies can be trimmed over like a hedge. Where an ivy has reached the top of its fence or wall and has begun to spread out, cut it hard back in early spring, using shears. You can do this every year. Virginia creepers can also be trimmed with shears when necessary (D).

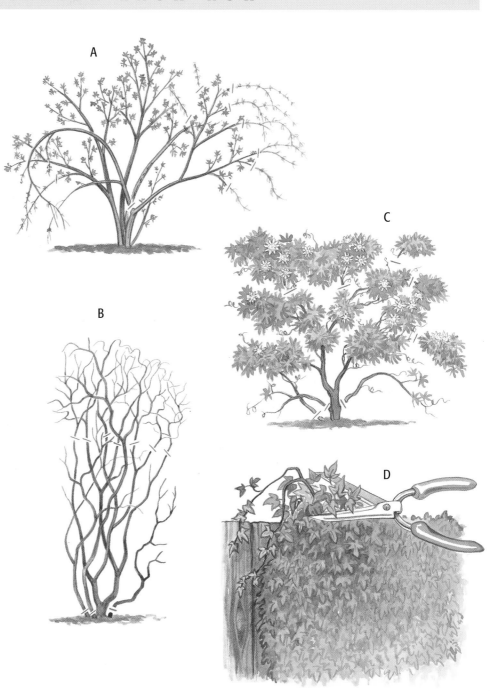

PRUNING NEW PLANTS

Most new climbers should have their stems reduced by half, either when they are planted or the following spring (except for climbing roses). In the first spring, pinch out the tips of the growing shoots to encourage the plants to send out new stems from low down, creating a strong framework.

Do not prune climbing roses for the first two years. Some climbing roses are sports from bush roses and may revert to their old form if they are cut back hard after planting. For more about pruning roses see pages 18–19.

To keep a honeysuckle flowering from top to bottom like this, prune after flowering.

HARD PRUNING

Some climbers can be cut hard back to ground level. *Clematis viticella* and its cultivars should be pruned regularly in this way. For full details of how to prune clematis, see page 21. Other climbers that can be cut hard back include *Aristolochia, Campsis, Lonicera* (honeysuckles), *Passiflora* (passion-flowers) and *Fallopia baldschuanica* (the Russian vine or 'Mile-a-minute' plant). Other overgrown climbers respond better to being gradually thinned out. *Parthenocissus tricuspidata* and other Virginia creepers can be cut back to stems no more than 5cm (2in) in diameter and will sprout again. Honeysuckles can be cut down to about 1.8m (6ft) if they have been allowed to grow unhindered for a number of years, otherwise they need pruning after flowering.

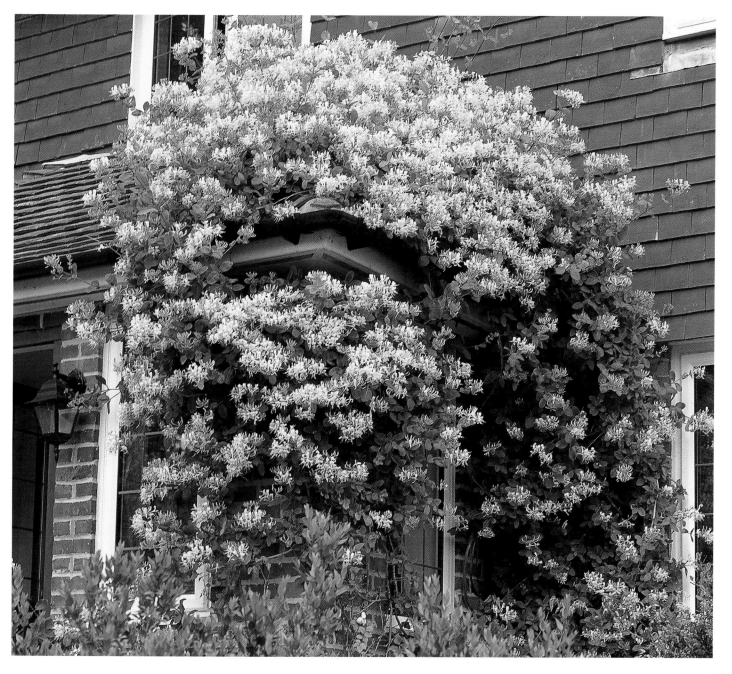

Caring for climbers

THERE IS NO NEED TO BE DAUNTED by growing and caring for climbers. The care of climbers is the same as the care of any other plant that you expect to last for a number of years. Below are some tips and advice on how to ensure that your climbers flourish.

ROUTINE CARE

• **Feeding** For the first few years, apply a general fertilizer in spring. Pelleted chicken manure, seaweed meal or a slow-release granular fertilizer are all clean to handle and easy to apply. Avoid using calcified seaweed meal if you are growing acid-loving plants.

• **Watering** All newly planted climbers will need regular and thorough watering in a dry year, just like other shrubs.

• **Mulching** Most climbing plants will benefit from regular mulching with well-rotted manure or compost each year in early spring. Apply the mulch when the soil is moist, adding a layer about 5cm (2in) deep. The mulch will help to retain moisture in the soil and will slowly break down into the soil to improve soil structure and fertility.

• **Winter protection** Many of the more colourful and exotic climbers are not fully hardy and may not survive a cold winter outside. There are many measures that you can take which will improve their chances of survival. The first and easiest thing to do is to mulch the roots heavily with anything you can get hold of, such as dry bracken, fallen leaves (which will need to be held in place with some form of netting), gravel, forest bark, coconut shell or a proprietary mulch. Cover an area at least 60cm (24in) from the base of the plant in all directions, to a depth of about 15cm (6in).

Wall plants can be protected by hanging straw matting from the wall over the entire plant. Alternatives are old curtains, rugs, bubble polythene, woven brushwood screening or horticultural fleece. If using any form of plastic sheeting, be sure to allow some ventilation. If possible, simply secure the material with bricks at the top and bottom of the wall. Remove winter protection as soon as the weather warms up.

COMMON DISEASES

Powdery mildew

Clematis, roses, grape vines (*Vitis*) and honeysuckle (*Lonicera*) are particularly susceptible. Leaves and shoots appear to be dusted with flour. Spray regularly with a proprietary fungicide. If plants are growing in a greenhouse, ensure good ventilation.

Blackspot

This is another fungal disease which causes large, noticeable dark brown or black patches on the leaves. Eventually the leaves turn yellow and fall off. These should all be carefully collected and burnt. Use a proprietary fungicide every 10 days, following the manufacturer's instructions. Some roses are resistant to blackspot and if it is prevalent in your area, you may need to replace your plants with resistant varieties.

Rust

Rust appears on roses as small orange pustules. Collecting the leaves and burning them is essential and you will also need to spray with a proprietary fungicide. Many manufacturers produce a combination spray for roses to cure blackspot, mildew and rust.

Clematis wilt

Clematis wilt is caused by a fungus which makes the whole plant collapse and die back at flowering time. It is very distressing but often the plant itself is not killed. Cut back the stems to ground level and spray with a copper-based fungicide. The plant may well shoot from the ground – if so, protect any new shoots from slugs. To prevent wilt occurring, plant clematis plants deeply.

Honey fungus

Honey fungus can attack woody climbers, including wisteria. The fruiting bodies, golden or brown mushrooms, grow at the base of the plant. White threads can be found in the ground and under the bark. Plants deteriorate and eventually die. Dig out the plant, including as much of the root as possible and burn it. Replant with a resistant climber.

Cucumber mosaic virus

Cucumber mosaic virus, which can affect all cucurbits, affects passion–flowers (*Passiflora*), stephanotis and hoyas as well. Infected plants produce warty, distorted fruits, blotched dark green and yellow. Leaves are undersized and distorted with mosiac patterns of yellow discolouration. Infected plants need to be destroyed immediately.

GARDEN KNOW-HOW

Getting a wisteria to flower

A wisteria grows quickly in its first years, producing plenty of handsome foliage, but often it will not flower until a woody framework has built up. This can take up to seven years in some cases, which is rather a long wait. Follow the instructions here to encourage it to produce its elegant clusters of scented, lilac blooms as early as possible.

If the wisteria is not flowering after 10 years, you may have a shy-flowering clone. You will have to face facts and either buy another plant and start again, or simply enjoy the leaves and twisted stems of the maturing plant.

1 Wisteria flower buds grow on short spurs, rather like apples and redcurrants. The aim of pruning is to persuade the plant to produce lots of short flowering spurs all along the main woody framework. Once the wisteria has covered the allotted space with woody branches, the new laterals which are produced each year should be cut back regularly.

2 Two months after flowering, prune the vigorous new growth back to 15cm (6in) from the main branch. This can be done every two weeks throughout the summer.

CARING FOR WISTERIA

Wisterias like a rich, medium loam. Where this is not available, ensure that the planting hole is half as big and half as deep again as suggested for other woody climbers and fill with enriched soil. Water heavily during the first summer. Wisterias last for many years and with a good start, need little attention after that except for pruning.

A wisteria needs lots of sunshine and a warm wall to help it flower well. In warm climates, wisteria can become a problem as it can be invasive.

ROOT PRUNING

Root pruning is occasionally advised for older wisterias that seem to be losing their flower power. In early spring dig a trench around the wisteria about 45cm (18in) deep and about 1m (3ft) away. Cut or saw the thick woody roots, being sure to leave the fibrous feeding roots untouched. Back fill the trench, firm the soil and water well.

Caring for roses

ROSA IS A VERY DIVERSE GENUS and some climbing roses will flourish with no feeding, no pruning and remain disease and pest free. Others are much less vigorous and demand a certain amount of cosseting. A good mulch around the roots with manure in winter and two feeds per season with a proprietary rose fertilizer (follow the directions on the packet exactly; more is not necessarily better), will keep most roses happy. Many climbing and rambling roses revel in hot sunshine and warmer climates: 'Climbing Lady Hillingdon', 'Marechal Niel', 'Paul Transon', *Rosa* × *beanii*, 'Royal Gold', *Rosa banksiae*, *Rosa* × *fortuneana* and 'Ramona' are just a few.

CREATING THE RIGHT EFFECT

Small-flowered roses look more informal than those with larger, showier blooms. For a position near the house, choose a large-flowered rose like 'Altissimo' or 'Compassion', but for a cottage-garden effect try 'Céline Forestier' 'Pleine de Grace' 'Dentelle de Malines' or 'Madame Alfred Carrière'.

PRUNING ROSES

Immediately after planting, cut back all the stems of roses to about 25cm (10in) to encourage a good, strong framework to develop. The only exception to this rule is climbers that are naturally occurring mutations of bush roses; these should not be pruned for two years as heavy pruning may make them revert to their bush form. After this initial pruning, adhere to the following pointers, depending on the rose type.

• **Ramblers** After planting, a rambler rose may take three years to flower but it will form a good root system during this time. Do not prune for two years after the initial cutting back. After this, ramblers should be pruned each year in late summer after flowering. Ramblers can be divided into two groups: the first group are very vigorous growers which produce new branches from the base which flower in the second year. As old branches produce less flowers, they can be cut to the base after they have flowered in late summer or early autumn and the new stems tied in (A). The second group, which are not repeat flowering, produce fewer new branches from the base; the old flowering stems should be cut back to a point where there is a strong replacement stem growing. Cut the stems back to the length you want them to be and then re-tie the stems to their support (B).

For a better screen, remove only a few of the older branches and cut one or two stems hard back to encourage new growth lower down. Many ramblers, like those that scramble over banks or through trees, need no pruning at all.

A

B

• **Climbers** Climbers produce their flowers on side stems and not on the structural branches. The structural branches should be trained immediately after the rose has been planted. Bend the branches to as near horizontal as possible without forcing them and tie them in place. Aim to create a balanced framework covering the designated area. Each year prune the flowering laterals by about two thirds in late summer and autumn (C).

C

• **Shrub roses** Encourage shrub roses to flower over the whole length of their stems by fanning the stems out horizontally if you are planting them against a trellis or fence. Shrub roses need little or no formal pruning. Cut back any branches that are inconvenient or damaged in late summer, after flowering (D). If you are growing them over an arch or pillar, prune one or two of the main stems so that they are shorter than the others; allow some to reach their full height, one to be about 1.2m (4ft) tall and another to be 60cm (24in).

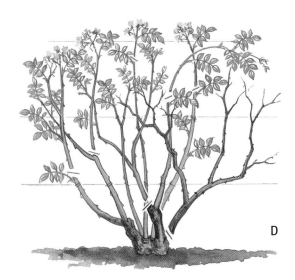

D

ROSES FOR DIFFICULT PLACES

If the only place you can grow roses is in semi–shade in difficult soil, such as heavy clay, very acid soil, drought-prone sandy soil or strongly alkaline soil, try growing the species roses. These are the roses that have evolved naturally and they are very tough. Choose from *Rosa pimpinellifolia*, *R canina* and hybrids of it, *R rubiginosa* and *R rugosa* – 'Blanche Double de Coubert' is a leggy white rugosa that can be used against a trellis.

Rambler roses are more successful than climbers in difficult soils, but the following tough cultivars are recommended:

'Climbing Cécile Brunner'
'Compassion'
'Constance Spry'
'Leverkusen'
'Maigold'
'Madame Alfred Carrière'
'Madame Grégoire Stachelin'
'New Dawn'
'Shropshire Lass'

The large clusters of intense pink flowers of *R.* 'American Pillar' can be overpowering in mixed company. Here, this tough and long-flowering rambler, shows to good effect against different greens.

Caring for clematis

CLEMATIS ARE AMONG THE MOST POPULAR CLIMBERS for temperate zones. The majority of species and cultivars are reliably hardy and sufficiently slender in growth to allow gardeners with even small gardens to include several.

You can find a clematis in flower on almost any day of the year and the range of colours is extensive. There are deep rich reds, yellows, almost blues, lavenders, purples and whites, and they are borne either as eyecatching individual blooms or in pretty clusters. Some of the species are scented, like *C. rehderiana* and *C. armandii*. Others make fine ground cover.

PLANTING CLEMATIS

Clematis like a cool root run – in nature they grow close to rocks or from the bases of shrubs or scrub – and it is important to try to replicate these conditions. This is easily done by shading the soil area with a stone or with small shrubs.

Water the plants in their pots before you start to prepare the soil as described on page 10. If the soil is poor replace it with a mixture of any proprietary compost, topsoil and a slow-release fertilizer such as bonemeal. On heavy clay soils, add grit and sharp sand to help drainage. On a sandy soil, increase the compost or add some very well-rotted manure to the bottom of the hole. If you plan to grow two clematis (or any other climbing plant) in the same hole, make the hole twice as deep, rather than twice as wide.

If the weather is very dry, fill the hole with water and let it almost drain away before planting the clematis. Plant the clematis with the top of the root ball 8cm (3in) deeper than it was in its pot. Fill the hole almost to the top with the soil and compost mixture and then water again. Top up the hole with dry soil and then mulch well on top. With our increasingly warm and dry summers, it is a good idea to insert a piece of pipe or plastic flower pot into the ground close to the plant roots to enable you to keep the roots thoroughly watered rather than the soil surface.

All clematis should be pruned back to the lowest pair of healthy buds in the first spring after planting to encourage them to become bushy at the base. Mulch each year in spring with well-rotted manure or compost.

Clematis montana is ideal for growing through a tree. Clematis should be planted at a distance from the tree trunk and guided towards it. It will need further support until it is well established through the branches.

PRUNING

Clematis are usually divided into three groups that need different pruning regimes. Whatever your clematis, if you buy a plant from a nursery or garden centre in full growth, do not prune until the following spring when all newly planted clematis should be pruned hard.

• **Group 1** (A) These are clematis which produce short flower stalks from the previous season's growth. They include *Clematis montana, C. alpina, C. armandii, C. chrysocoma, C. cirrhosa* and *C. macropetala*. No regular pruning is necessary. They only need tidying up immediately after they have finished flowering. *C. montana* can be cut hard back if it has outgrown its space and you can do this a little later in the summer. Take care when cutting into old hard stems, however, as the plant may die.

• **Group 2** (B) These are the early-flowering, large-bloomed cultivars, such as 'Belle of Woking', 'Duchess of Edinburgh', 'Nelly Moser', 'Beauty of Worcester', 'Marie Boisselot', 'Dr Ruppel', 'Barbara Jackman', 'Daniel Deronda' and 'The President', which flower before mid-summer. Prune back dead and damaged stems to a strong pair of buds in late winter or very early spring. On a wall or trellis these large-flowered clematis need to be tied in carefully to support the flowers, but if they are growing up a tree or shrub, this will probably not be necessary.

• **Group 3** (C) These late-flowering clematis produce their flowers in clusters at the end of the new season's growth. They belong to the Jackmanii, Orientalis, Texensis and Viticella groups and include 'Hagley Hybrid', 'Niobe', 'Perle d'Azur', 'The Princess of Wales', 'Gravetye Beauty', 'Ernest Markham', 'Ville de Lyon' and 'Minuet'. In late winter and early spring, cut back each stem to just above the first pair of strong buds that you come to from the ground.

There are about a thousand clematis varieties available, with new ones appearing each year, so it is impossible to list each one and say how it should be pruned. Nursery catalogues and plant labels usually indicate which pruning group a particular clematis belongs to, so ask when you buy a plant. Remember, too, that it is not a disaster if you do not prune. The clematis will still flower, but not so well and often only on the higher branches.

A

B

C

Choosing a climber

THE MAJORITY OF CLIMBERS will grow in any reasonable soil; most books recommend a moisture-retentive, free-draining, moderately fertile loam in sun or partial shade for most plants. Unfortunately these ideal conditions are the exception rather than the rule. Most of us struggle to grow plants in less than perfect soil and it is useful to know what climbers are likely to do well in the conditions and aspect we can offer. There are some that must have an acid soil, while others do better in an alkaline soil. Some climbers will tolerate drought, others a damp soil.

Whatever the soil type or the aspect, prepare the soil carefully first, adding organic matter, such as manure, compost or rotted grass cuttings, to increase fertility, aid moisture retention and open up the texture. Most climbers will be in place for a long time and need a good start.

CLIMBERS FOR ACID SOIL

If your neighbours grow heathers and rhododendrons, your garden probably has acid soil. It is worth buying a soil testing kit from a garden centre to test the pH just to make sure. Acid soil has a pH of less than 7.

Asteranthera ovata
Berberidopsis corallina
Billardiera longiflora
Hydrangea seemanni
Kadsura japonica
Lapageria rosea
Mitraria coccinea
Mutisia oligodon, M. decurrens
Schisandra chinensis, S. rubriflora,
    S. sphenanthera
Tropaeolum speciosum

CLIMBERS FOR ALKALINE SOILS

Most plants that will grow in alkaline soil will do well in neutral or even slightly acid soils. Alkaline clay is difficult to work but is more fertile than thin chalk soil. Add organic matter to both when preparing the ground, but add several handfuls of coarse grit to the alkaline clay as well. Alkaline soil has a pH value of more than 7.

Actinidia kolomikta
Akebia quinata, A. trifoliata,
    A. × pentaphylla
Celastrus orbiculatus
Clematis sp.
Clianthus puniceus
Euonymus fortunei
Hedera colchica, H. hibernica
Holboellia coriacea
Humulus lupulus 'Aureus'
Hydrangea anomala ssp. petiolaris
Jasminum officinale
Lathyrus grandiflorus, L. latifolius
Lonicera
Parthenocissus henryana
Rosa sp.
Rubus
Schizophragma hydrangeoides,
    S. integrifolium.
Solanum crispum 'Glasnevin',
    S. jasminoides 'Album'
Trachelospermum
Vitis coignetiae, V. vinifera 'Purpurea'

CLIMBERS FOR HEAVY SOIL

Heavy, clay soils are often highly fertile but prone to waterlogging in winter and cracking in summer. Add plenty of organic matter and grit when planting climbers. Other materials that can be worked into the soil for advantage are coarse sand, ashes, leafmould, manure, compost and some lime. If the soil is a very heavy clay, consider replacing the soil in the planting hole with loam-based compost. Test the pH of the soil if you hope to grow acid-loving plants.

Ampelopsis
Aristolochia macrophylla
Campsis grandiflora, C. radicans,
    C. × tagliabuana 'Madame Galen'
Celastrus orbiculatus; C. scandens
Clematis (most species)
Decumaria barbara, D. sinensis
Fallopia baldschuanica
Humulus lupulus 'Aureus'
Hydrangea anomala ssp. petiolaris
Lathyrus grandiflorus,
    L. latifolius
Lonicera
Menispermum canadense
Pileostegia viburnoides
Rosa 'Albéric Barbier', R. banksiae,
    R. filipes 'Kiftsgate', R. 'Maigold',
    R. 'Paul's Himalayan Musk',
    R. 'Zéphirine Drouhin'
Rubus
Smilax rotundifolia
Solanum crispum 'Glasnevin'
Vitis coignetiae
Wisteria

CLIMBERS FOR FREE-DRAINING SOIL

Climbers on the borderline of hardiness survive better in a well-drained soil, but many of these also need a high degree of fertility. Do not omit to feed and mulch plants in free-draining sandy soils. Check whether the soil is acid or alkaline.

Anredera cordifolia
Campsis grandiflora, C. radicans,
   C. × tagliabuana 'Madame Galen'
Clianthus puniceus
Cobaea scandens
Cucurbita
Ercilla volubilis
Euonymus fortunei
Hedera
Holboellia coriacea, H. latifolia
Jasminum officinale
Lycium chinense
Muehlenbeckia complexa
Parthenocissus henryana,
   P. quinquefolia
Passiflora (some species)
Periploca graeca
Schizophragma hydrangeoides
Solanum crispum, S. dulcamara
   'Variegatum', *S. jasminoides*
Trachelospermum asiaticum,
   T. jasminoides
Tropaeolum
Wisteria

CLIMBERS FOR COLD PLACES

Many climbers come from parts of the world where the temperature can drop very low but survive because hotter summers ripen the stems well. In more temperate regions they may not flower or fruit as prolifically.

Actinidia kolomikta
Ampelopsis glandulosa
   var. *brevipedunculata*

Apios americana
Celastrus scandens
Clematis aethusifolia, C. alpina,
   C. montana
Euonymus fortunei var. *radicans*
Fallopia baldschuanica
Hedera colchica, H. helix
Jasminum nudiflorum
Lathyrus latifolius
Menispermum canadense
Parthenocissus quinquefolia
Rosa canina, R. setigera
Rubus fruticosus laciniatus,
   R. phoenicolasius
Schisandra chinensis
Tripterygium regelii
Vitis amurensis, V. 'Brant',
   V. coignetiae, V. labrusca
   'Concord', *V. vinifera* 'Ciotat'
Wisteria floribunda

CLIMBERS FOR SHADE

While plants usually need sun to flower well, honeysuckles and some leafy climbers prefer shade.

Euonymus fortunei
Fallopia baldschuanica
   × *Fatshedera lizei*
Hedera

Climbing hydrangea
Hydrangea anomala ssp. petiolaris.

Hydrangea anomala ssp. petiolaris
Lonicera brownii, L. × heckrottii,
   L. sempervirens, L. × italica,
   L. × tellmanniana,
Parthenocissus henryana,
   P. tricuspidata 'Lowii'
Pileostegia viburnoides
Rosa 'Félicité Perpétue', *R.* 'Madame
   Alfred Carrière', *R.* 'Madame
   Grégoire Staechelin', *R.* 'Mermaid'
Tropaeolum speciosum

CLIMBERS FOR COASTAL GARDENS

Salt laden winds are a problem in coastal gardens but there are some climbers that can withstand them.

Actinidia arguta
Campsis radicans
Clematis indivisa, C. montana
Fallopia baldschuanica
Hibbertia scandens
Hydrangea anomala ssp. petiolaris
Muehlenbeckia complexa
Parthenocissus tricuspidata,
   P.t. 'Lowii'
Smilax lanceolata
Vitis labrusca

Boston Ivy
Parthenocissus tricuspidata.

COLOURING WITH CLIMBERS

*F*or many people, flower colour is what makes a garden. This is particularly so in parts of the world where winters are damp and grey and light levels are low. The gentle sunlight, even in summer, makes some colours appear harsh. People long for colour but feel uneasy about using it because too often the colourful garden can be a confused glare of competing shades. Frequently, too, people forget to include what may be the main colour of the garden, the bright green of grass, when they are designing their colour schemes.

In contrast, in hot climates the brilliant sunshine makes bright colours look vivid and alive. The flame orange *Pyrostegia venusta* that will cover a chain-link fence to such brilliant effect in Australia, or the vivid magenta bougainvillea that swamps white painted cottages in Greece, look brash in soft northern light and, anyway, need a conservatory to flower really well.

C. Tropaeolum speciosum has vivid red flowers in late summer and shows to perfection against a yew hedge.

Using colour

IF YOU WANT YOUR GARDEN TO LOOK EXCITING, classically smart, romantic or simply bigger, then colour can do it for you and climbers will do it quicker than any shrub. Colours can create many effects in the garden – you can cool an arid garden or cheer up a shady one just by choosing colours carefully.

If you want to make the bottom of your garden seem further away, then plant climbers in receding colours such as soft blue or mauve. For a garden where the view is particularly important, the colouring can continue the scene. For example, in a seaside garden, keep to the colours of the sea and use complementary colours sparingly. Brilliantly coloured climbers at the end of the garden in front of a view will bring the eye to a stop and spoil the effect, whereas some gentle greens will lead the eye on.

COLOUR AND SPACE

There are some simple axioms that are always worth keeping in mind:

• White flowers jump forward and appear to be closer than they really are, particularly in full sun. Use them to highlight attractive features or elements you want to bring to the fore.

• White and pale flowers will appear to glow in shade; they can be used to light up dark corners to good effect.

• Deep colours such as dark red and purple create "holes" in the planting. They appear to recede into the foliage.

• Soft blues and greys look further away than they really are and add to the apparent distance. Use these colours at the bottom of a small garden to make the garden appear larger.

• Hot, strong colours, such as scarlet, orange and yellow appear to reduce distance and look closer than they really are.

Clematis 'Duchess of Edinburgh' leaps out of the picture, taking the attention from *Solanum crispum* 'Glasnevin' which, on its own, is quite an eye-catcher too. Later, when the clematis has finished flowering, the solanum will come into its own.

DESIGNING WITH COLOUR

The natural landscape is usually made up of one colour, or a harmony of colours over a wide area, like a bluebell wood or an autumn scene. If there are many colours together, as there may be in a meadow, then the colours are like a kaleidoscope with shifting blues, reds and yellows harmonized amongst the dominant green of the grass. Both these scenarios create a pleasing and subtle effect.

However, if those same colours are separated into dense blocks or drifts as they may be in garden plantings, the individual colours start to compete with each other, all trying to claim attention at once. This can be exciting in the right surroundings, for example in a public park, but not in a garden designed to be a place of peace and tranquillity.

There are three main ways of designing with colour in the garden:

• **The Italian method** In brilliant light an Italian garden can seem almost black and white, with dark evergreens and pale stone. There is just a small amount of brilliant colour, with a few pots and tubs of flowers.

• **The natural way** Nature keeps one colour or a harmony of colours dominant over a wide area or if there are lots of colours, then they are broken up into kaleidoscope patterns.

• **Using plants like paints** This idea uses colour more deliberately and artistically. Gertrude Jekyll did this in the early part of the 20th century in England, using subtle progressions of colour, for example from pale blue to white to palest yellow and pink, then through the yellows to orange and red. The colours are strong in the centre of the bed, but "in good harmonies, never garish". In South America, Roberto Burle Marx designed gardens and flower beds made up of bold shapes in vivid contrasting colours, which look like modern paintings.

THE COLOUR WHEEL

The colour wheel or colour circle was devised in the mid-19th century and the colours are arranged so that complementary colours fall opposite to each other. Many designers and flower arrangers find this helpful in planning their colour schemes and it can be used to plan a border too.

Complementary colours

These are the colours that fall opposite to each other in the colour wheel, such as red and green, purple and orange or blue and yellow. When used together in a colour scheme, each heightens the effect of the other. For example, the pink of almond blossom in spring looks better when seen against a grey–blue conifer than it does against the bright green of young leaves. A flash of orange seen in a woodland becomes more vivid and the green of the trees appears more intense. However, proportion is important. The quieter colour should be the prevailing one, the bright one a spot of contrast.

Harmonious colours

Harmonious colours are those that sit next to each other on the colour wheel, such as blue and purple, or yellow and orange. These do not contrast as complementary colours do,

but produce a more subtle effect. The most popular harmonious colour schemes are pink, purple and blue, or the hot colours of red, orange and yellow.

If you want a very natural effect and a garden that will blend with the surrounding countryside, then you need to stick to pale harmonious colours, particularly in spring. Many native trees and shrubs of northern Europe have either green or white flowers – and these fit wonderfully with the fresh green of new leaves, the white and pale yellow of the earliest bulbs and herbaceous flowers. As the greens get darker later in the year, then brighter colours work well with them. If you are planning a town garden, green and white are cool and restful all summer through. On the other hand, enclosed gardens in built up areas can be enclaves of vivid colour and dramatic foliage, unrelated to their surroundings. The choice is yours.

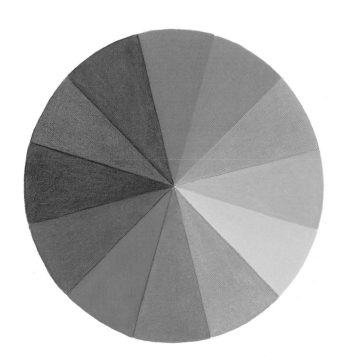

The colour wheel shows how different colours relate to each other and can help in planning a colour scheme.

SINGLE COLOUR SCHEMES

Ever since Vita Sackville West devised her White Garden at Sissinghurst, Kent, single colour gardens have been popular. It is not too difficult to create a one–colour border and the restriction in colour stops the planting looking fussy and gives it a unity which is advantageous in a small garden.

Choosing colours

WHETHER YOU WANT TO CREATE A SPECIFIC MOOD IN YOUR GARDEN or have a particular problem that you need to solve, colour is one of the most important considerations. Below are lists of selected plants, ordered by colour group, to give you some ideas as to the effect that different colours have and which plants you can use to get that splash of colour.

BLUE AND PURPLE

Blue flowers give a cooling effect and create a sense of distance. Finding true blue climbers, however, is not easy and most blues have a tinge of purple about them. Purple covers a wide range of colours, including mauves, lavenders, lilac and violet. Purple and violet are rich, sumptuous colours with a fair amount of pink in them, while lavenders and lilac are cool and, like blue, have a distancing effect.

Aconitum hemsleyanum
Clematis alpina 'Francis Rivis'
Clematis 'Lasurstern'
Clematis 'Perle d'Azur'
Cobaea scandens
Codonopsis convolvulacea
Ipomoea indica, I. tricolor
Lathyrus

Passiflora caerulea
Plumbago auriculata
Sollya heterophylla
Thunbergia grandiflora
Tropaeoleum azureum
Tweedia caerulea
Wisteria

RED AND PINK

Red flowers are always eye-catching; use them to draw attention to a particular feature or to distract from an ugly area. There are several good red roses, and in tropical regions there are some wonderful reds. Pink flowers have a pretty, old-fashioned effect, though different pinks vary hugely from deep purple-pinks to rich red-pinks and soft pastel pinks. If you are aiming for a cottage garden effect, try growing some pink, small-flowered climbers to create the desired effect.

Actinidia kolomikta
Asteranthera ovata
Berberidopsis corallina
Clematis 'Ernest Markham'
Clematis 'Niobe'
C. 'Nelly Moser'
Clianthus puniceus
Distictis buccinatoria
Eccremocarpus scaber
Gloriosa superba
Ipomoea lobata
Ipomoea quamoclit
Jasminum beesianum
J. × stephanense
Lathyrus latifolius
L. odoratus
L. rotundifolius
Lonicera × brownii 'Dropmore Scarlet'

L. × italica
L. periclymenum 'Serotina'
Maurandya barclayana
M. erubescens
Metrosideros carmineus
Rhodochiton atrosanguineus
Rosa (see pages 32–33 for examples)
Tropaeolum majus 'Crimson Beauty'
T.m. 'Crimson Velvet'
T.m. 'Darjeeling Red'
T.m. 'Empress of India'
T.m. 'Forest Flame'
T.m. 'Hermine Grashoff'
Tropaeolum speciosum

Left: The fascinating detail of *Passiflora caerulea*, the hardiest of the passion flowers.

Right: The vigorous white flowered rambler rose, 'Rambling Rector', is trained so that it looks like a spectacular weeping tree, impossible to overlook. The small flowers ensure that it fits well into this country garden.

YELLOW AND ORANGE

Yellow is a warm colour and brightens up a garden, especially in the winter. In cooler regions, yellow is a welcome sunny colour. It can look brassy and garish however and is often rather perversely "out of fashion". This also applies to orange, another warm colour, useful for adding a tropical effect or bringing a border to life.

Allamanda cathartica

Bomarea caldasii

Campsis

Clematis orientalis 'Bill
  Mackenzie'

C. tangutica

Eccremocarpus scaber

Jasminum nudiflorum

L. etrusca

L.e. 'Donald Waterer'

L.e. 'Michael Rosse'

L.e. 'Superba'

Lonicera × heckrottii

L. × heckrottii 'Gold Flame'

L. hildebrandiana

L. japonica 'Halliana'

L. sempervirens f. sulphurea

L. × tellmanniana

L. tragophylla

Thunbergia alata

Tropaeolum majus

T. peregrinum

T. tuberosum. var.
  lineamaculatum 'Ken Aslet'

WHITE AND CREAM

White flowers can light up corners in shady areas and they are useful for toning down some of the more brash colours. Some whites are more penetrating than others. Stephanotis, for example, is a very stark white, while the white wisteria can be palest pink or have a hint of lavender. Creams can vary from ivory to pale buttery yellows and have a softer effect than pure white.

Araujia sericifera

Clematis alpina 'White
  Columbine'

C. montana grandiflora

Clianthus puniceus 'Albus'

Codonopsis convolvulacea
  'Alba'

Hydrangea anomala petiolaris

Jasminum officinale

J.o. affine

J.o. 'Argenteovariegatum'

J. polyanthum

Passiflora caerulea 'Constance
  Elliott'

Rosa (see pages 32–33 for
  examples)

Schizophragma hydrangeoides

S. integrifolium

Trachelospermum jasminoides

Wisteria brachybotrys

Wisteria sinensis 'Alba'

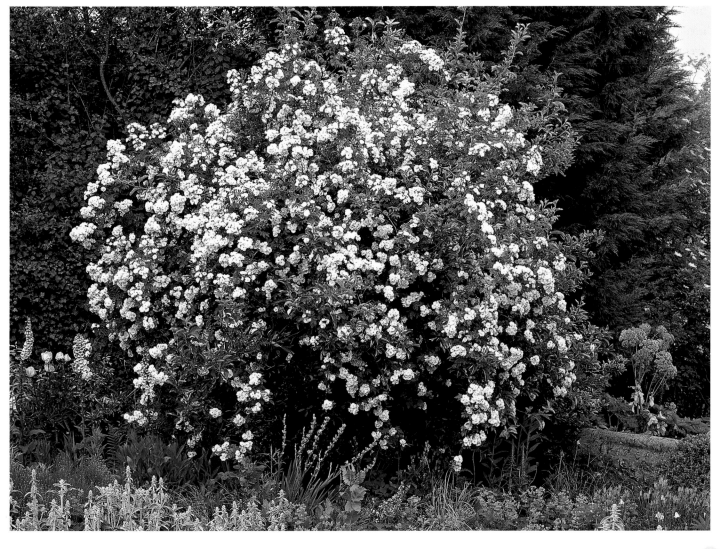

Greens

GREEN IS THE MOST PREVALENT COLOUR IN THE GARDEN and comes in many shades and, importantly, many textures. Capability Brown and other landscape designers used the different greens of foliage alone to frame or hide a feature or to draw the eye onwards.

The effect of leaf size on a plant or how it actually climbs, changes the way the plant looks. Large leaves appear instantly exotic while small leaves and a scrambling habit are more cottage-garden in style: think of honeysuckle or wild roses.

The surfaces of leaves vary as well, not only from plant to plant but from season to season. Ivy, an often neglected plant, has bright glossy leaves in spring but later in the year the leaves darken and can seem dull and drab. If you want to get light in a corner, use climbers with glossy evergreen foliage which will shine and reflect every bit of light there is.

HANDSOME LEAVES AND AUTUMN TINTS

The *Parthenocissus* are wonderful foliage plants with large, shapely leaves which will densely cover a wall or fence. As an added bonus, they take on glorious autumn colours in shades of orange, flame and crimson before the leaves fall. The most common plants are the Boston ivy (*Parthenocissus tricuspidata*), the Chinese Virginia creeper (*P. henryana*) and the Virginia creeper (*P. quinquefolia*). These are all self-clinging climbers.

Parthenocissus quinquefolia, the well known Virginia Creeper, has fresh green new leaves in spring which turn into rich shades of orangey-red in autumn.

IVY

Ivy is perhaps the most underrated of climbing plants. Its very ubiquity, its hardiness and ease of cultivation and its reputation for destroying walls means that this handsome and worthwhile plant is often ignored when climbers are being considered. Yet it has a number of uses, and when it is used and grown well, it can be truly eye-catching.

Sound walls, whether brick, stone or stucco, will not be damaged by ivy. Most small town gardens, enclosed patios or yards, could benefit from the rich permanent green of ivy leaves. In the early part of the year the fresh glossy green of their new leaves is as heartening as any spring flower.

Ivy can be used to outline an arch, create a false pillar or completely cover an area. Retaining walls built of breeze blocks can be disguised with ivy. It can be combined with other climbing plants like *Clematis armandii*, or the annual, (in temperate zones), *Eccremocarpus scaber*, for colour, or you can have a group of mixed ivies. *Hedera helix* 'Oro di Bogliasco' is colourful, with yellow centred leaves and pink stems. Avoid the plain native *Hedera helix* which can eventually become invasive. Choose instead one of the many distinctive varieties which are much less rampant.

Hedera colchica is believed by many to be the finest of all ivies. The leaves can be 20cm (8in) long and it is a strong grower. The variegated forms *H. colchica* 'Dentata Variegata' and *Hedera colchica* 'Sulphur Heart' ('Paddy's Pride') are especially eye-catching. The Irish ivy, *H. hibernica* has broad leaves and is another good grower.

FOLIAGE FOR SHELTERED SPOTS

Other evergreens for year-round effect include the slightly tender *Trachelospermum jasminoides* and *T. asiaticum*. They both need the protection of warm walls to flourish. They have fragrant white flowers in clusters at the ends of their shoots and need tying to supports. Although grown for their flowers, the leaves are particularly good. *Stauntonia hexaphylla*, with dark glossy leaves and small clusters of white, fragrant flowers in spring, is another example of a slightly tender plant which is well worth trying. In a good year, it even produces purple–red fruits. *Solanum crispum* 'Glasnevin' is semi–evergreen in mild winters as is its cousin, the not quite as hardy *Solanum jasminoides* 'Album'. These are both really grown for their flowers but the foliage is a bonus. 'Glasnevin' has clusters of showy blue–purple potato flowers, while those of *S.j.* 'Album' are white.

Pileostegia viburnoides, a member of the hydrangea family, is evergreen and quite hardy. It needs a warm wall to flower well but is reputed to thrive on a sheltered north wall. The handsome leaves are narrow and corrugated. The flowers are small and white, in flattish panicles.

FOLIAGE AND FLOWERS

The evergreen Japanese honeysuckles, *Lonicera japonica* 'Halliana' and *L. henryii* are, like ivies, underrated and under-used plants. *L.j.* 'Aureoreticulata' was much favoured a few years ago for its variegated leaves, green netted with yellow, but its flowers are inconspicuous. *L.j.* 'Halliana' is quick growing and vigorous and the florets in the leaf joints, which are white, fading to yellow, are highly scented and produced over a long period in summer. It will grow almost anywhere and will soon cover a tree, pergola or trellis. *L. etrusca* 'Superba' has bolder flowers in creamy yellow but it is slightly tender and needs a warm spot.

MAKING PATTERNS WITH EVERGREENS

Many evergreen climbers can be trained so that they form patterns on a wall, rather than covering the whole wall. Plants such as ivy, *Euonymus fortunei radicans*, *Ficus pumila* and *Periploca graeca* can be trained into squares, diamonds or even free–forms against plain walls. This idea is especially suitable on an attractive wall which you do not want to entirely cover with foliage. It is very easy to do by pinching out shoots and new growth that are not going where you want them to.

Ivies (*Hedera* sp. and cvs) can be easily trained to create dramatic effects. Here the ivy is grown to form a criss-cross pattern, which breaks up, but does not conceal a length of brick wall. To make this pattern, use two plants in each planting hole, training one diagonally to the left and the other to the right. Ivy needs to be supported for the first year until it puts out aerial roots.

Using roses for their colour

FOR MOST PEOPLE, ROSES ARE IN THE PREMIER LEAGUE when it comes to colour. They are the most popular climbers, grown for their scent and their superb flowers in shades of deep purple, through red to pink and white, and from white to cream, yellow, orange, vermilion and almost brown. They are mid-summer flowers and the often intense colours balance with the deeper green of summer leaves.

SOME RECOMMENDATIONS

• To make the bottom of the garden seem further away, choose *Rosa* 'Veilchenblau' which is the bluest of climbing roses, or pale pinks and soft yellows.

• If the views from the garden are not good, choose dramatic roses that will attract attention inside the garden. Large white roses like *R.* 'Climbing Iceberg' jump forward and are ideal for distracting the eye from an ugly building.

• A pergola or line of pillars clad with bright red or yellow roses will also draw the eye and create a striking feature.

• If you want roses that are pale and cool, choose 'Albéric Barbier' which is yellow in bud and opens to a creamy white, or 'New Dawn' which is the palest flesh pink and seems to go with everything except other "blue" pinks.

• Sumptuous dark red roses, such as *R.* 'Guinée', a climbing hybrid tea with a delicious scent, are perfect for romantic plantings and they need to be seen close up. Beware, however, 'Guinée' is difficult to grow and can be mean with its flowers. 'Climbing Etoile d'Hollande', another rich red rose, is easier, but its brilliance does not have quite the same romantic appeal.

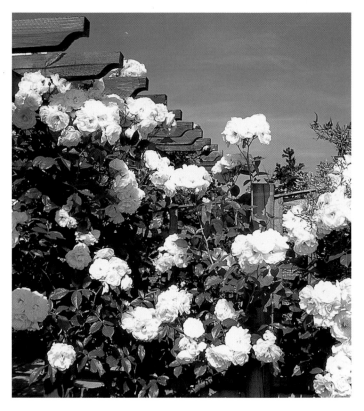

Rosa 'Climbing Iceberg', grabs attention with its clusters of large white flowers over a long season.

RED
'Altissimo'
'Château de Clos-Vougeot'
'Climbing Crimson Glory'
'Macdub' (Dublin Bay)
'Parkdirektor Riggers'
'Paul's Scarlet Climber'
'Tess of the D'Urbervilles'

WHITE and CREAM
'Albéric Barbier'
'Félicité Perpétue'
R. filipes 'Kiftsgate'
'Madame Alfred Carrière'

'Rambling Rector'
'Wedding Day'
'White Cockade'

YELLOW
'Céline Forestier'
'Clarence House'
'Emily Gray'
'Gloire de Dijon'
'Golden Showers'
'Graham Thomas'
'Leverkusen'
'Maigold'
'Mermaid'

ORANGE
'Climbing Bettina'
'Crown Princess Margareta'
R. foetida 'Bicolor'
'Harquanne' (Breath of Life)
'Joseph's Coat'
'President Herbert Hoover'
'Schoolgirl'

PINK
'Albertine'
'Aloha'
'Baltimore Belle'
'Bantry Bay'

'Blairii No. 2'.
'Chaplin's Pink'
'Constance Spry'
'Madame Grégoire
   Staechelin'
'New Dawn'
''Zéphirine Drouhin'

PURPLE
'Archiduc Joseph'
'Bleu Magenta'
'Rose-Marie Viaud'
'Veilchenblau'
'William Lobb'

A colonnade of colour

A colonnade is a useful way of dividing a garden visually and giving some height, without losing light or a feeling of space. It is basically a series of columns linked together, over which climbing plants can be trained. Rambling roses are particularly suited to this type of structure. Architectural colonnades are seen in formal rose gardens, with brick columns and wooden cross pieces. A wooden colonnade linked with rope will do the same thing more cheaply and makes a handsome garden feature.

To make this structure you will need pressure-treated timber uprights at least 15 x 15cm (6 x 6in) square or very sturdy rustic wood poles at least 15cm (6in) in diameter. They need to be about 3m (10ft) in length. You will also need bulky rope, about 6cm (2in) in diameter, to link the uprights. Decide how far apart you want your uprights to be, calculate how much rope you need and add sufficient length to make a good knot on each end of the rope.

1 Drill holes through each upright large enough to thread the rope through, about 7cm (3in) from the top.

2 Arrange the uprights 2–3m (7–10ft) apart and, ensuring the drilled holes are in alignment, set them in holes about 50cm (20in) deep and 30cm (12in) square (A). Pack rubble around the base of each upright and prop them up straight with temporary battens. Tamp a concrete mix hard around them and leave to set.

3 Thread the rope through the holes in the uprights so that it hangs down a little, creating an attractive scalloped effect. When doing this, bear in mind that the rope will probably lengthen a little over time. Knot firmly in place (B).

4 Cover the uprights with a capping of lead, galvanized metal or a wooden finial, to prevent rain seeping in.

PLANTING THE ROSES

When making planting holes, position them so that the prevailing wind will blow the plants towards the uprights rather than away (see pages 10–11 for more details on planting). Twist the roses round the uprights as this encourages the production of flowering shoots. Rose stems need to be trained into a suitable position while they are still young and pliant. Tie them on to the uprights with plastic rose ties, string or raffia.

CHOOSING ROSES

Rambling roses are best suited to growing over a colonnade. Choose from the following:

'Alexander Girault'
'François Juranville'
'Ghislaine de Feligonde'
'New Dawn'
'Phyllis Bide'
'Tour de Malakoff'
'Veilchenblau'
'William Lobb'

A

B

Colour through the year

IT IS EASY TO HAVE A COLOURFUL GARDEN IN SUMMER, too easy sometimes for the garden can be full of summer flowering climbers with no room for climbers that are interesting at other times. To extend the interest through into autumn, winter and early spring takes more planning, particularly if there is a colour theme to the garden.

Evergreen Climbers for Temperate and Warm Temperate Regions

• *Asteranthera ovata* A clinging climber with small leaves in opposite pairs and glowing red tubular flowers.
• *Berberidopsis corallina* Has leathery green leaves and hanging clusters of rich red globular flowers.
• *Clematis armandii* Has large, elliptical leaves and clusters of small, white scented flowers in late winter, early spring.
• *Clematis cirrhosa*, *C.c.* var. *balearica* and *C.c.* 'Freckles' Have attractive fern–like foliage and small creamy white bell–shaped flowers. The two variants are spotted inside, 'Freckles' being the most vivid.
• *Euonymus fortunei* Often seen as a shrub with glossy, deep green leaves but it will produce roots on the stems as ivy does, when it has reached the top of its support. There are small orange seeds in pinkish cases in autumn.
• *Hedera* Self–clinging climber with several important species and hundreds of cultivars.
• *Pileostegia viburnoides* A root climber with long, oval leaves and flattened heads of creamy white flowers in autumn.
• *Stauntonia hexaphylla* Has dark glossy leaves and small clusters of white, fragrant flowers in early spring. In a good year, it even produces purple–red fruits.

The large leaves of *Hedera colchica dentata* 'Variegata', the Persian Ivy, are bright and cheerful all year round.

• *Trachelospermum* Has glossy green leaves in opposite pairs. *T. asiaticum* is shy flowering, with jasmine–like white flowers fading to yellow. *T. jasminoides* has larger, very fragrant flowers but is not so hardy.

Spring

• *Akebia quinata* A vigorous twining climber with pale green leaves and unusual chocolatey purple flowers.
• *Clematis alpina* A slender climber with pendulous, lantern–shaped flowers in blue, white or pink.
• *Clematis macropetala* As the name indicates, the bell–shaped blue, pink or white flowers on these species are semi double; the centres full of small, narrow petals.
• *Clematis montana* White or pink four petalled flowers smother this very vigorous plant in late spring, early summer, every year.
• *Rosa banksiae* 'Lutea' – almost thornless rose, with small, double pale yellow flowers in hanging clusters.

Summer

• *Clematis* sp. (large-flowered) Summer flowering hybrids with flowers that can be 20cm (8in) across. They are usually in shades of white, pink, lavender, purple and deep red.
• *Jasminum* sp. A family containing well–known climbers such as *Jasminum officinale*, the common white jasmine, a twiner bearing pure white scented flowers in clusters from mid–summer to mid–autumn. *J. polyanthum* with pink buds is not so hardy.
• *Lathyrus odoratus* Sweet peas are hardy annuals that climb using leaf tendrils. There are many different colours and they are easy to grow from seed.
• *Lonicera* sp. Climbing honeysuckle species and cultivars have long tubular flowers in pairs, sometimes borne singly as in the Japanese honeysuckle and sometimes in clusters, as in the native honeysuckle, *L. periclymenum* and *L.p.* 'Belgica' with red and yellow flowers.
• *Rosa* sp. Summer is the optimum time for climbing and rambling roses of all colours, from bluish lilac to white, cream, yellow and red.

Autumn

• *Ampelopsis glandulosa brevipedunculata* Vigorous vine with bright blue berries. *A.g.b.* 'Elegans' has white variegated leaves.

• *Celastrus orbiculatus* Twiner with red seeds in yellow–lined seed cases in autumn.

• *Clematis sp.* There are three climbing clematis species that flower from late summer on into autumn. They are *C. orientalis*, *C. rehderiana* and *C. tangutica*. They all have small yellow flowers. *C. viticella* cultivars, like 'Purpurea Plena Elegans' and 'Etoile Violette' will flower until early autumn.

• *Solanum crispum* 'Album' White potato flowers and mid–green leaves, flourishes until the frosts.

• *Tropaeolum speciosum* Scarlet flowers in summer, purple bracts and blue berries in autumn.

• *Vitis coignetiae* A vigorous ornamental vine with large rounded leaves, mid–green on top and covered with reddish hairs underneath. In autumn the leaves turn rich apricot to red.

Training a colourful climber round a pillar

Create a wonderful feature in the garden by growing two beautiful climbing roses around a pillar. You may be lucky enough to find a stone pillar in an architectural salvage merchants or have a tree with a straight bare trunk already. If not, a piece of wood about 20cm (8in) in diameter and between 2–3m (6–9ft) long can be set firmly in concrete in the ground or a very simple brick column can be constructed.

1 Select two young climbing roses, ensuring that the main stems are very pliable. Make a planting hole on either side of the pillar and plant the roses (A). See page 33 for more guidance on how to plant a rose.

2 Guide the leaders of one rose to go clockwise and the other anti-clockwise so that the stems cross over, making a pattern of squares over the pillar (B). Fix in position on a wooden pillar using lead-headed nails or, if the pillars are stone or brick, use proprietary plastic ties with discs that stick firmly to any surface (C).

3 Training the stems so that they are more horizontal than vertical encourages the branches to produce flowering laterals all along their length rather than just at the top (D).

4 Remove unwanted main stems unless, more economically, you want only one type of rose on your pillar (E). The rose will have more than one stem and it is quite possible to train them in opposite directions to get the same lattice effect as when using two plants. When the main stem has reached the top of the pillar, pinch the top back (F).

5 Each year, after flowering, cut back the laterals to two or three outward facing buds. Mulch the base with well-rotted manure in winter (G).

CHOOSING PLANTS

Do not choose roses that are too vigorous. *R.* 'Zephirine Drouhin', *R.* 'White Cockade', *R.* 'Little Rambler', *R.* 'Phyllis Bide' or *R.* 'Paul's Scarlet Climber' are good choices.

Pairs of clematis look very effective when grown this way but the pillar would need to be covered with netting for the clematis to attach themselves to. Most hybrid clematis would be suitable (for suggestions, see page 66).

To extend the season of interest to a rose covered pillar, add an early flowering clematis like *C. alpina* 'White Columbine', *C.a.* 'Francis Rivis' which is blue, fluffy blue *C. macropetala* or *C.m.* 'Markham's Pink' and even a late flowering viticella hybrid such as *C. texensis*, 'Duchess of Wales'. The rose stems will provide good support for the clematis.

DESIGNING WITH CLIMBERS

*F*or most of us, garden design seems to be a rather frightening subject, best left to the experts. Much design, however, is simply problem solving, particularly in a modestly sized garden. What to hide, what to draw attention to, how to add height to a flat site, how to manage the difference between levels – these are all problems that can be solved by using climbing plants on different supports. When planning a garden layout, scale and proportion are important. There should be a pleasing relationship between the length, breadth and height of features and their relationship to the elements around them. Even in a small enclosed garden, you need to think on a larger scale than at first seems necessary. Features are more often too small rather than too big. To get the scale right, use bamboo canes or off-cuts of wood to represent the new features you are planning and try them in the garden for size and position. Designers learn to visualize the scale of things or they draw scale plans, but most of us need to see something in place before we know what it will look like.

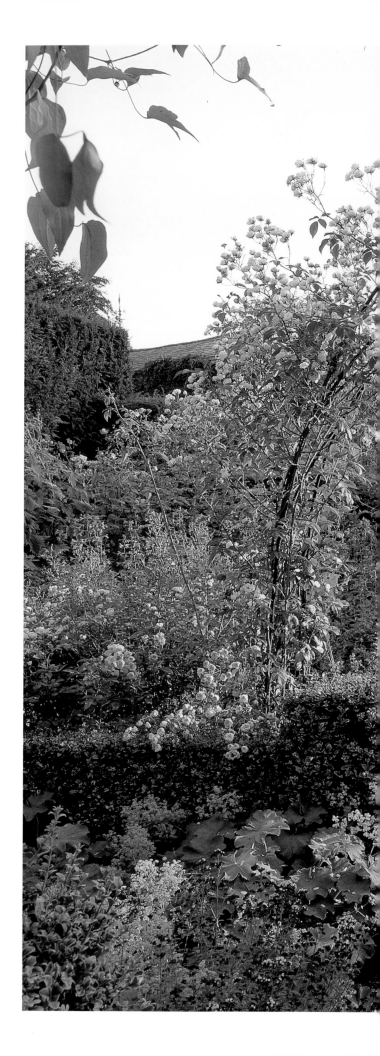

Rose covered arches frame a pretty fountain silhouetted against a background of sober yew. The series of arches is planted with *Rosa* 'Seagull' and are sufficiently far apart to allow plenty of light through enabling *Nepeta* 'Six Hills Giant' to flourish.

Arches and arbours

ARCHES CAN BE USED AS EYE-CATCHERS, but they work better if they are positioned to frame a view, a path or a small feature which can be as modest as a pot of summer bedding. An arbour is a shaded bower, usually a wooden or metal structure clothed in climbing plants which offers a private place to sit and relax.

ARCHES

Simple frame arches covered in climbers are a quick way of bringing height into a garden; this avoids the dense shade that a tree of the same height would give and you can plant close to the uprights. An arch will also determine how people look at space. If you want people to look down your path or at a piece of sculpture, frame the approach with an arch.

You need to be able to stand well back from an arch to look through it properly, so in a small garden place the arch at the far end of the garden, over a sundial, bird bath or other ornament.

In a town garden, an arch should be architectural in style, perhaps with trellis to support climbers. Avoid rustic arches which look better in a country garden or well away from the house. The town garden arch needs to look attractive by itself, but not too flamboyant or it will detract from the climbing plants that clothe it.

Framing a view

Where you are framing an attractive view, use less flamboyant climbers which are beautiful close to, but at a distance do not distract from the picture they are supposed to frame.
• *Celastrus orbicularis* has bright fruits and leaves in autumn, at a time of the year when you might like to draw the interest inside the garden because the leaves have fallen from trees outside your boundary and revealed surroundings which are a little humdrum.
• *Clematis rehderiana* This has small pale yellow bell-shaped flowers in clusters, and should be cut down in early spring to about 30cm (12in) from the ground.
• *Humulus lupulus* and *H.l.* 'Aurea' These are fast growing herbaceous perennials that twine. The lobed maple-like leaves are rough to the touch.
• *Solanum jasminoides* 'Album' has small leaves and delicate white potato flowers in late summer. It needs to be cut back every winter except in milder areas, but is vigorous and soon makes up for lost time.

Brick gate posts and an iron frame make a sound structure for the vigorous and floriferous clematis, *C. Jackmanii*.

CHOOSING PLANTS FOR ARCHES

As the arch is a frame to a "picture", it is more effective if it is planted either with dark leaves or with bright flowers that appear to jump forward. It should draw first the eye and then the footsteps towards it. From the north facade of a house, an arch covered with ivy or other dark evergreen will make the sunny area beyond look even more tempting. Plant the area beyond with receding colours and grey-leaved plants. On the south side of a house, looking towards the end of the garden, which will be the shady north side of the boundary fence or wall, plant the arch with strong bright colours that jump forward and the garden through the arch with quieter colours, to make the distance beyond the arch seem longer.

Making a temporary arbour

Create a temporary arbour with planting boxes and trellis supports. If you have just moved into a house and are not yet sure what you want to do with the garden or perhaps are just renting, you can make a temporary arbour to shelter a garden bench using readily available materials and quick growing annual climbers. Choose a site that gets sun in the morning or late afternoon.

1 Choose two square planting boxes, 30 x 30cm (12 x 12in) or bigger, and trellis panels slightly narrower that are made with two extensions at the bottom. Most garden centres will stock these.

2 Put stones or broken pots into the bottom of the boxes and support the trellis with them.

3 Put the boxes in place before you fill them up with good quality soil-based potting compost (A). Add slow-release fertilizer, following the manufacturer's instructions.

4 Plant annuals or climbers like sweet peas, black-eyed Susan, morning glories, *Rhodochiton atrosanguineus* or canary creeper, to climb over the trellis (see pages 56–57). Complete the planting by adding scented bedding plants such as heliotrope to the boxes (B).

A

B

5 Link the two side pieces with a piece of trellis, the same width as the side pieces, across the top (C), and, if you choose, another broader piece of trellis across the back. Wire the pieces together securely.

PLANTS FOR ARBOURS

Scented plants are the best choice if you intend to sit and relax under the arbour – choose exotic white jasmine, roses or honeysuckle. The planting should not be too dense, as the arbour should be inviting rather than dark and spidery. Arbours can also be formed from plants alone, by shaping and training trees or shrubs such as yew.

If you want something discreet, try *Ampelopsis megalophylla* which has long leaves and will create a very private place or the evergreen *Holboellia coriacea* which is strongly scented. It has shiny leaves and two sorts of flowers which appear at the same time: the male flowers are purple-green bells in clusters, while the female flowers are larger and greenish-white with a purple tinge. Although the plant will survive temperatures of –10°C (50°F), it is best to mulch the plant well in winter if the arbour is not in a very sheltered position.

C

Arcades and pergolas

AN ARCADE IS A SERIES OF ARCHES. Like a colonnade or series of columns it can look confused if not well planted. Pergolas are very similar to arcades, but while an arcade has a curved top, that of a pergola is always flat. There must be a strict relationship between width, height and spacing for these features to look balanced.

SITING A PERGOLA

Pergolas and arcades are large features and may be too big for a small garden, particularly if erected down the middle. At first a pergola seems to add height, but it also creates a strong horizontal axis with the repetition of the columns. In a large garden, a pergola can make a wonderful feature providing a support for many climbing plants.

Like a colonnade, a pergola can make a useful division if built across the garden. It can also be erected against the back or sides of a house or the side walls or fences of a garden so as to create a cloister effect. If the pergola is to be built near the house, it looks better if it is more architectural and the materials are related to those of the house with, for example, brick columns in the same type of brick as that of the house. If possible, lay a paved or gravel path underneath a pergola as little will flourish in the deep shade.

Remember that a pergola, like an arch, works as a picture frame and it should always lead to something, perhaps a garden seat or an urn of flowers.

Climbers can be planted quite close to the uprights of a pergola. Unlike trees or walls, the soil at the base of a pergola is unlikely to be particularly dry.

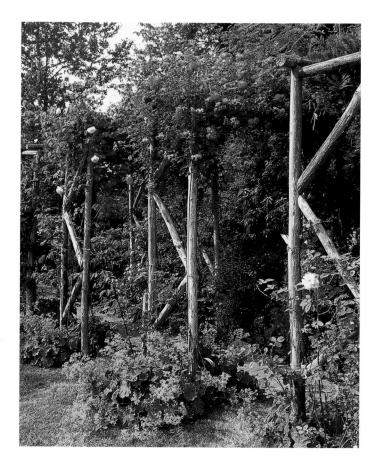

A charming rustic pergola supports a variety of pink and red roses.

CLIMBERS FOR PERGOLAS

A large pergola can support some magnificent plants. Apart from some of the larger roses, the classic pergola plant is a wisteria. For a few weeks each year the long racemes of mauve or white fragrant flowers hang down inside the pergola creating a magical cave.

Other good plants to consider are:

• *Actinidia kolomikta* Which has green leaves with pink and white tips.

• *Akebia quinata* Which has unusual brownish purple flowers that have a vanilla scent in spring.

• *Clematis sp.* Almost any clematis can be paired with other climbers on a sturdy pergola as well.

• *Humulus lupulus* 'Aureus' The golden hop.

• *Jasminum officinale* Has pinnate green leaves and small, white heavily-scented flowers, luxuriantly borne.

• *Lonicera × heckrottii* Has showy panicles of yellow flowers with red buds.

• *Passiflora caerulea* 'Constance Elliot' The lovely white passion flower is perfect for a pergola in a warm area.

• *Periploca graeca* The silk vine is a strong grower and has dark, shiny foliage. The brownish-purple flowers are interesting but smell unpleasant and are followed by pods containing seeds, each of which has a long tuft of silky hairs.

• *Schisandra rubriflora* With brilliantly coloured red flowers.

• *Solanum crispum* 'Glasnevin' With purple potato flowers.

• *Vitis coignetiae* The crimson glory vine, has wonderful autumn colouring.

Building a pergola

A pergola built against a house wall is easier and cheaper to make than a free-standing feature and creates a simple cloister effect. Three uprights are the minimum number for a small pergola and they should be placed about 1.8m (6ft) apart at their centres. Cross-pieces join the uprights to the wall opposite where they are fixed to a timber house plate. The uprights should be placed no further than 2.5m (8ft) from the side of the house. The uprights should be made of 10 x 10cm (4 x 4in) pressure-treated timber, 3m (10ft) long. You will need six crosspieces made of 10 x 2.5cm (4x1in) timber, 3m (10ft) long. The house plate should be made of 10 x 5cm (4 x 2in) timber, approx. 3.8m (12ft) long. You will also need a piece of timber to act as a brace, 10 x 2.5cm (4 x 1in), approx. 3.8m (12ft) long.

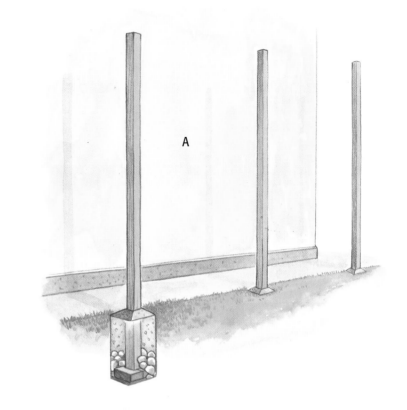

1 Dig a hole for each upright, 30cm (12in) square and 60cm (24in) deep. Put two engineering bricks in the bottom of the hole and then put the posts in. Pack some hardcore or stones around the bases of the posts to hold them in place. Make sure they are vertical, level and in alignment with each other and support with temporary battens. Tamp a concrete mix hard around the uprights, bevelling the top of the concrete so that it slopes away from the post in all directions. Leave to set (A).

2 Fix the timber plate to the house wall, ensuring the top of the plate is at exactly the same height as the top of the uprights. Drill through the timber into the house wall and secure firmly in place with coach bolts (B).

3 Cut the timber brace to fit the total width of the structure and fix it to all three uprights on the inside of the structure, about 5cm (2in) down from the top, using coach bolts. This will hold the pergola square.

4 Cut the six cross pieces to length, so that they will extend just beyond the uprights. You may also like to jigsaw a curve into one end of each cross-piece to create an attractive finish. Cut a 5cm (2in) deep notch on four of the cross pieces at the point where they will slot over the brace. Use coach bolts or nails to fix each cross-piece firmly in place on either side of each upright. Drive nails in at an angle to fix the end of each cross-piece to the wall plate, or use galvanized fixings (C).

TRAINING ROSES

Remember, if you are using climbing roses on your pergola, twist the main shoots round the uprights, fixing them with plastic rose ties or string while they are still pliable. Cut any side shoots back to three or four buds each spring to encourage flowering and keep the roses under control.

Focal points

CLIMBING PLANTS CAN BE USED IN many different ways to create focal points, some more permanent than others. Obelisks and pillars constructed from timber or trellis make good semi-permanent features in a garden. They can be planted with permanent plants such as roses or honeysuckle, or with more transient plants such as *Lathyrus grandiflorus*. Climbers trained as standards can be either a fixed or temporary feature depending upon where they are planted and ivy topiary in a pot is a simple way to create a feature that can be moved around in the garden.

PLANTS FOR OBELISKS

• *Thladiantha dubia* is from the same family as the cucumber and has yellow flowers and heart shaped leaves.
• The maurandyas and lophospermums, twining snap-dragons, are also good in this situation. *Lophospermum* *erubescens* (syn. *Asarina erubescens*) and *Maurandya barclayana* can be grown from seed, but need well-drained soil and a sheltered spot. These are sometimes described as asarina in seed catalogues.
• *Codonopsis convolvulacea*, with lilac, five-petalled flowers needs dappled shade.

GARDEN KNOW-HOW

Ivy topiary

Ivy can be used to make "topiary" focal points. It can be grown round a wire frame inserted into a large pot. These frames are usually painted dark green, come in a variety of shapes and sizes and are readily available. Alternatively, you can make a simple shape from chicken wire, stuffed with moss.

1 Insert the legs of the frame or the wire construction into a container filled with good compost. Make sure the container is not too flimsy.

2 Plant an ivy plant by each upright and firm it well in, adding more compost if necessary. Water well (A).

3 You will need to tie the ivy stems to the uprights until they begin to mesh together. Pinch out stems that are too wayward (B).

4 When the frame has been completely covered by the ivy, maintain the shape by trimming the ivy with a pair of shears.

How to make a standard wisteria

Standard roses, where flowers and leaves develop from a straight, bare stem of up to 2m (6ft) high are well known. Many other plants can be trained in this way including wisteria. Standards are useful because in full flower they make an eyecatching feature while allowing other plants to be grown right beneath them. The Chinese wisteria, *W. sinensis*, or one of its cultivars, is the species to grow because of the spectacularly long racemes of flowers.

1 Plant your wisteria, either in a 45cm (15in) pot of John Innes No. 3 compost, or in the ground in a prepared planting hole (see page 10). Support the main stem with a sturdy cane (A). Water well.

2 Remove any other shoots. When the main stem has grown to 50cm (20in) beyond the top of the support, remove the tip.

3 Lateral shoots should then appear along the whole length of the stem. Shorten these side shoots back to four or five leaves (B), but let the shoots at the top grow to the length you want. These will form the "umbrella" at the top of the stem. Leaving a few leaves on the stem strengthens it.

4 After two years or so, when the upper branch system, the ribs of the umbrella, are well developed, you can remove all the short branches on the lower part of the stem. The wisteria will need to be kept staked (C).

A
B
C

OTHER CLIMBERS TO BE TRAINED AS STANDARDS:

Bougainvillea

Jasminum azoricum

Lonicera japonica

Mandevilla splendens

Petrea volubilis

Stephanotis floribunda

Trachelospermum
jasminoides

STANDARD ROSES

The following climbing roses make excellent standards:

'Albéric Barbier'

'Albertine'

'Dorothy Perkins'

'Excelsa'

'Emily Grey'

'Félicité Perpetué'

'Francois Juranville'

'Golden Glow'

'Minnehaha'

'Sanders White'

Temporary eye-catchers

EVEN IN THE SMALLEST GARDEN, you can create temporary focal points by using pots containing a wigwam of canes supporting exotic tender climbers. Group them on the patio in the summer or drop them in to fill gaps in beds and borders, where they will add instant height and colour.

There are lots of very showy tender climbers which will bring an exotic feel to the garden. If you don't have anywhere to protect them from frost in the winter months, such as a conservatory or greenhouse, then choose annual climbers instead which will flower profusely through the summer and die off in the autumn such as sweet peas and black-eyed Susan.

You can use these temporary features either singly or in groups, creating a rhythm in the garden border. Placed symmetrically in twos and fours they give a very formal effect, while in threes the effect is more relaxed.

PLANTS TO CHOOSE

• Sweet peas (*Lathyrus odoratus*) are well-known annuals which provide summer colour and perfume.

• *Ipomoea quamoclit* is an annual morning glory with bright crimson flowers.

• The quick-growing black-eyed Susan (*Thunbergia alata*) is an annual with vivid orange flowers and a black eye.

• *Passiflora* 'Allardi' is a perennial which has blue, pink and white flowers and is scented.

• *Senecio macroglossus* 'Variegatus' has variegated ivy shaped leaves and white daisy flowers. It is also perennial.

• *Sollya heterophylla*, the Australian blue-bell is a perennial with pale green lanceolate leaves and sky-blue bell-shaped flowers, 1cm (½in) long.

• *Ipomoea indica*, the evergreen, perennial morning glory has rich purple blue flowers, ageing to reddish pink.

• *Chorizema cordatum*, the Australian flame pea, has bunches of small pea flowers in orange with a purple keel. It is perennial.

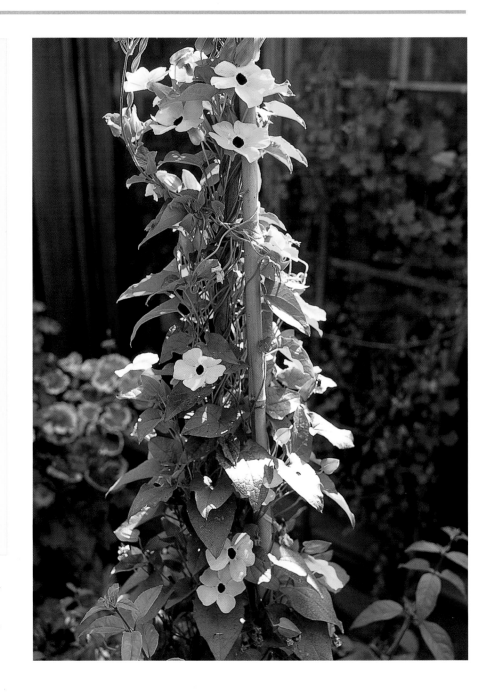

The annual climber, Black-Eyed Susan, *Thunbergia alata*, is ideal for growing up the simple supports, such as bamboo canes, to make a temporary focal point. Black-eyed Susan is widely available in shades of apricot, ivory and yellow but seed mixtures can now be bought which produce a good proportion of red blooms.

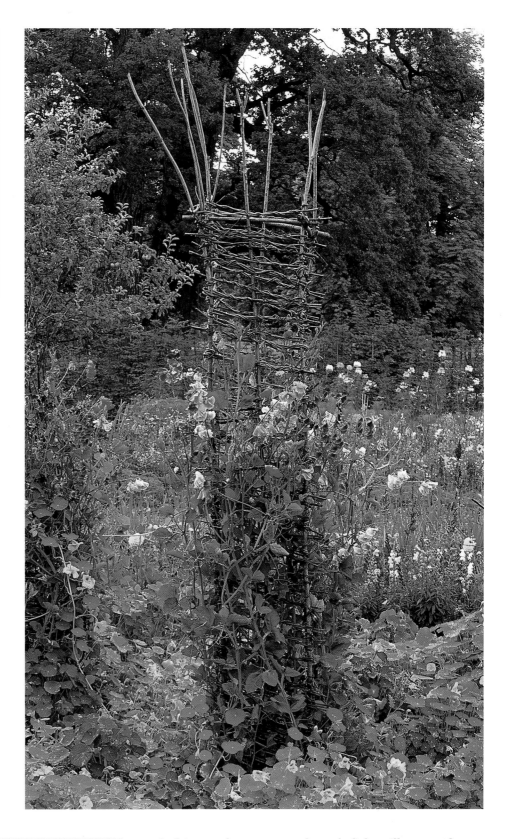

This wicker structure has a modern shape but fits in well to these informal surroundings. Here it is forming a support for sweet peas but later in the summer the nasturtiums rampaging around its base, could well be persuaded to take over. Many annual climbers prefer a rough textured support such as these twisted twigs, to smooth plastic, bamboo or iron.

MAKING A TEMPORARY SUPPORT

• To make a temporary support for short–lived or tender climbers, even one post driven into the ground will do.

• Other very simple structures to make or buy are bamboo or woven willow wigwams or obelisks. These bring a rustic feel to the garden, but the shapes are graphic enough to look at home in most situations.

• Architectural supports, such as obelisks, pillars or columns are also suitable.

• Try pyramids of softwood or painted or stained trellis.

• Metal supports are attractive. They are usually wrought iron, but these days even aluminium or galvanized zinc are often used.

• Perspex makes a very modern support for climbers but can only be obtained from specialist designers.

PRACTICAL SOLUTIONS

*S*ome climbing plants are very good at concealing things. These are not necessarily the most eye-catching of climbers but they have the advantages of good, dense foliage and many are quick growing. Often, in a garden, covering an unattractive but immovable feature or blocking out ugly surroundings is as important as putting something beautiful in it. Climbers do a splendid job of growing up, over or even along the ground, adding texture, colour and interest.

A well-established covering of *Wisteria sinensis* and *Lonicera x americana* turns a sober brick wall into a beautiful garden feature.

Screens

CLIMBING PLANTS ARE IDEAL FOR SCREENING. Screens out of doors can be as varied as screens indoors. They can be either dense, completely concealing something, or fine like a veil. Whatever type of screen you want to create, climbing plants are preferable to the frequently chosen Leyland's cypress (× *Cupressocyparis leylandii*). There is, of course, the equivalent of a Leyland's cypress among the climbing plants and that is *Fallopia baldschuanica*, the Russian vine or mile-a-minute plant. On the whole, these rampant plants should be avoided in the garden – there are other toughies in the climbing world that can be as effective but on a much smaller scale.

QUICK ANNUAL SCREENS

There are many lovely fast-growing plants which will create colourful screens for the summer months. Many of the plants sold as annual climbers are, in fact, perennials which come from warm climates. They grow so fast and flower in the first year so they can be used as annuals in cooler places. Treat them like any other tender bedding plant and put them in position when all danger of frost has passed in your area.

Most annual climbers are fairly insubstantial plants: to make a dense screen plant them very thickly in well prepared soil. Enriching the soil too much, however, tends to make the plant produce too much leaf at the expense of flowers, but this may be an advantage in some situations.

CHOOSING ANNUAL AND HERBACEOUS CLIMBERS

• The cup and saucer vine (*Cobaea scandens*) is a very fast growing perennial with large, intriguing flowers. The bell flowers could be described as a murky purple and there is also a pale green form, sold as 'Alba'. If cobaea is grown as an annual it should be started off early. Seed can be tricky to germinate because it really needs to be sown fresh. Sow the seeds on their edge singly in 8cm (3in) pots. They will need potting on and pinching out and then staking in cooler climates before it is time to put them out in the garden.
• The canary creeper (*Tropaeolum peregrinum*) grows to about 1.5m (5ft) and has small yellow fringed flowers. The effect is rather informal and the flowers do not have a great impact from a distance but the screening quality is good; the leaves are prettily shaped like those of a fig. To ensure a long season of flower and leaf, buy two packets of seed and sow one batch indoors in mid-winter and the other packet out of doors at the end of spring when the soil has warmed up. Look out for blackfly and cabbage white caterpillars.

• The Chilean glory flower (*Eccremocarpus scaber*) has orange-red tubular flowers. There are other colours available including red (*E.s. carmineus*), yellow (*E.s. aureus*) and pink (*E.s. roseus*). This plant climbs using lots of tiny tendrils. In cold areas, it is killed in the winter but in warmer regions it survives in the ground, even if cut back by frost. In very warm areas it flowers all year.
• *Rhodochiton atrosanguineus* has long, tubular dark purple flowers with a pagoda top in reddish-purple and always attracts attention. It can grow to 1.5m (5ft) but is suitable for veiling rather than screening. Sow the seeds under glass in early spring.
• The kudzu vine (*Pueraria montana lobata*) grows from tuberous roots and will grow to 10m (30ft) in a season. It makes a good screen or cover for buildings. It needs a hot wall to flower well, however. The flowers are purple and grow in bunches.

SWEET PEA SCREENS

The best-known annual climber is the sweet pea (*Lathyrus odoratus*). Seedsmen have been hybridizing sweet peas since about 1865 and there have been hundreds of varieties, although not all have lasted to the present day. As the flowers have become larger and the colour range wider, so the perfume for which the sweet pea is so loved has become fainter, so be sure to choose a scented variety. The recently reintroduced 'Matucana', which was one of the earliest varieties, has small bicoloured purple and reddish purple flowers and a particularly strong scent.

You can sow sweet peas, as you would edible beans and peas, along rows of bamboo canes to make a free-standing screen. This would be a good, yet easy and cheap way of screening off a vegetable plot. Alternatively, grow them up the plastic netting that is sold as pea and bean netting, attached to a fence or trellis.

This heavenly blue *Ipomoea sp.* or Morning Glory, will twine happily round anything.

GARDEN KNOW-HOW

Success with sweet peas

Much of the mystique about growing sweet peas is aimed at enthusiasts who grow them for exhibition. Growing sweet peas to make a screen is quite simple.

1 Sow the seeds in late winter or early spring singly in 8cm (3in) pots in seed compost (A). Some experts advise filing down the seed coats until the white of the seed shows through to help them germinate. Older varieties do not always need this.

2 Put the pots in a warm place or, if possible, in an electric propagator at 15ºC (59ºF). Remove from the propagator as soon as the seeds have germinated and place in a cold frame or other light, frost-free but unheated place.

3 When the plants are about 8cm (3in) high, pinch out the tops to make the plants bushier. Plant out autumn sown plants in mid-spring and spring sown plants in late spring, spacing them about 25–30cm (10–12in) apart (B). The further apart the plants, the better the flowers. The soil should be moisture-retentive and have plenty of well-rotted manure or compost added to it. Sweet peas will happily stand partial shade.

4 Sweet peas will provide plenty of flowers, but they should be removed as they begin to fade. The formation of seed pods must be prevented if the plant is to continue flowering. If this is done, you should get flowers for at least three months. Keep picking them to keep the plants flowering.

PERENNIAL PEAS

If you want to be really economical, choose perennial sweet peas rather than the annual variety, so you get a show of flowers year after year. Try *Lathyrus latifolius* in pinky-purple, *L.l.* 'Albus' in white or. *L.l.* 'Rosa Perle' in pretty pink. They will flower the first year if you sow the seed early enough, but will flower even better the second year. Other species worth trying are *L. chloranthus* which has flowers somewhere between lemon and lime, 'Lord Anson's Blue Pea' (*L. nervosus*) which has attractive light blue flowers, and *L. grandiflorus*, the everlasting pea with rich pink and red blooms.

A

B

Hiding an eyesore

EYESORES like oil tanks, old sheds, unattractive chain link fencing or brand-new larch lap fences can soon be blended into the garden or completely disguised with vigorous climbing plants. There are a number of very different plants that can be used, from rambling roses to Japanese honeysuckles.

HEAVY-DUTY COVER

The Russian vine (*Fallopia baldschuanica*) is one of the first climbers gardeners think of when faced with the problem of an ugly structure in their garden. When it has not only covered that unsightly shed, but completely filled it as well, they often regret their choice so treat it with extreme caution. It is tough, fast growing and trouble free, with hanging clusters of tiny white flowers in late summer. It will grow in any soil in sun or shade. If only it wasn't so rampant, it would be the perfect plant for an unenthusiastic gardener. Give it a miss though, unless you have a factory to hide.

RAMBLING ROSES

Some of the more vigorous rambling roses are perfect for covering up unsightly features. The following all have pretty, small white flowers and do a good job covering large structures in big gardens in the summer: 'Rambling Rector', 'The Garland', 'Mannington Cascade', 'Seagull' and *R. filipes* 'Kiftsgate'. It would be worth trying the following slightly less vigorous ramblers for their coloured flowers: 'Treasure Trove' is creamy apricot, while 'Hiawatha' is a red single flower with a white eye and 'Chevy Chase' has large clusters of small deep crimson double flowers.

COVERING WITH CLEMATIS

Clematis montana will cover a small building in three or four years, giving a spectacular and fragrant display of flowers in late spring, early summer. *C.m. grandiflora* has larger white flowers, *C.m. rubens* has pink flowers, *C.m.* 'Freda' has deep cherry-pink flowers and bronze foliage and 'Tetrarose' has large pink flowers. Pruning is not normally necessary, but if they are getting too overgrown for comfort, prune immediately after flowering. 'Bill Mackenzie' with its large flowers is another good clematis for concealing unattractive structures, as is the late-flowering *C. orientalis*. It has pretty yellow flowers, followed by fluffy seedheads.

LESS WELL-KNOWN PLANTS

There are many other good covering plants which are less well known. They include:

• Moonseed (*Menispermum canadense*), a woody climber with blue-black berries in autumn. The handsome, circular leaves can be 20cm (8in) across. It spreads by underground suckers and makes a good summer covering for unsightly sheds.

• Japanese honeysuckle (*Lonicera japonica* 'Halliana'), the related *L.j.* 'Hall's Prolific', and *L. henryi* are evergreen and very hardy.

• *Vitis coignetiae* is a vine grown for its enormous leaves which colour pink and apricot in the autumn.

Vitis coignetiae is among the most vigorous of vines and has large heart-shaped leaves which turn shades of brilliant red, pink and apricot in autumn. It makes a good screen.

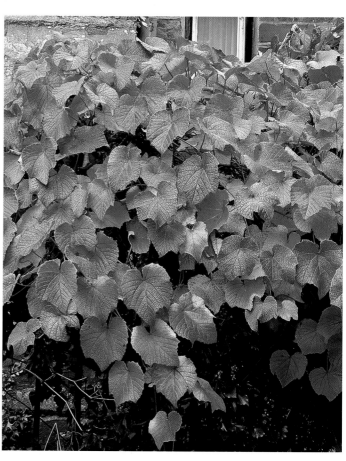

• The golden hop (*Humulus lupulus* 'Aureus') is a fast, strong grower with attractive leaves. The leaves are quite rough, however, and if the plant is grown near a path, the stems can catch passersby unawares. This is a herbaceous climber which dies down in the winter months.

• Ivies, of course, are good at concealing things.

• Dutchman's Pipe (*Aristolochia macrophylla*) has interesting curved green flowers, but these are often hidden by the leaves. The heart-shaped leaves get larger as they age. This plant must have moisture-retentive soil.

COVER FOR CHAIN-LINK FENCES AND RAILINGS

For a perennial cover for chain link fences and railings, the two Japanese honeysuckles *Lonicera japonica* 'Halliana' and *L.j.* 'Hall's Prolific' are both good choices. The tendril climber, Boston ivy (*Parthenocissus tricuspidata*) also makes a very dense screen and will cover very large areas. The honeysuckle has small but very scented flowers and the Boston ivy has good autumn colour.

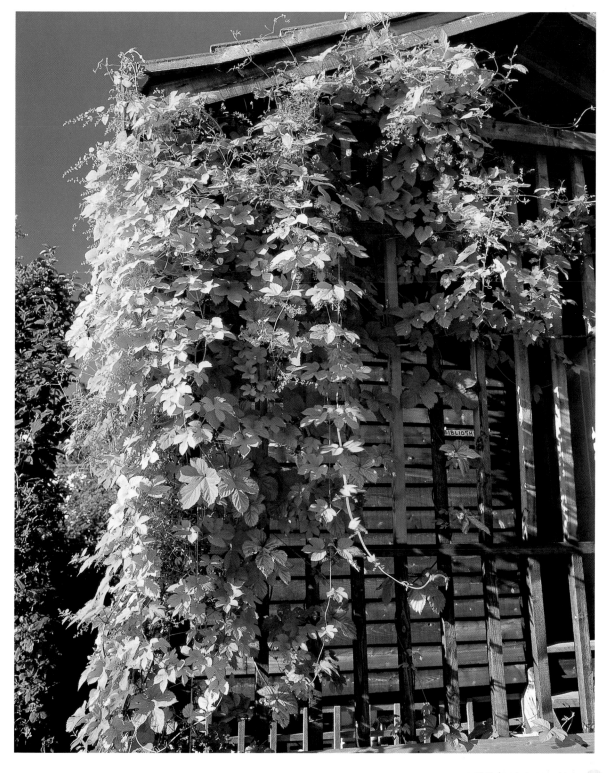

The golden form of the climbing hop plant, *Humulus lupulus* 'Aureus' grows well on a trellis. The twining stems need support and the new shoots should be woven through the trellis when they first appear each spring. This vigorous perennial has hanging clusters of "hops" in autumn and is a good choice for covering unsightly objects.

Walls and fences

MANY CLIMBING PLANTS make an attractive cover for walls and fences of all types and are especially valuable if the boundary underneath is less than appealing. For solid walls in good condition, whether concrete, brick, stone or render, self-clinging climbers such as ivy and Virginia creeper can save the bother of drilling to attach wires or trellis. Some however, even ivy, can take a little time to cling properly and will benefit from support until they start to cling themselves.

If your wall or fence is relatively attractive, you can still enhance it with climbers, just choose less dense or vigorous plants. In these situations the climber should merely enhance its support, so pick the really pretty plants with a good show of flowers.

SELF-CLINGING CLIMBERS FOR WALLS

Members of the hydrangea family are among the best self-clinging climbers, but they can be slow to get established. It is worth waiting, however, for they are magnificent plants and trouble free. *Hydrangea seemannii* has large, dark evergreen leaves and exciting heads of white flowers. It is not, however, as hardy as *Hydrangea anomala petiolaris* (the climbing hydrangea), which has similar flower heads made up of tiny, white fertile flowers surrounded by larger sterile flowers.

The flowers of the schizophragma (*Schizophragma hydrangeoides* and *S. integrifolium*) have elegantly oval sepals at the end of each stem. *S. hydrangeoides* 'Moonlight' has leaves flushed with silver, while *S.h.* 'Roseum' has pink flowers.

Pileostegia viburnoides is evergreen and has small white flowers in panicles about 15cm (6in) long. Another hydrangea relative, *Decumaria barbara*, will cling to a tree trunk but needs some support on a wall. The plant is deciduous or semi-evergreen and the flowers are scented but do not have the showy bracts. *D. sinensis* is evergreen but less tolerant of cold.

PLANTS FOR MOIST SHADE

Ercilla volubilis is an evergreen climber that likes moist shade and lime-free soil. It is good for a north wall, provided it is not too windy and the small oval leaves will give a dense cover. The stems are long, gradually turning woody and the whitish-pink flowers are produced in spikes in spring.

Asteranthera ovata is another evergreen that needs the same conditions. It has small crinkled leaves and large red trumpet flowers from summer onwards and tends to spread sideways rather than grow upwards.

The flower colour of *Campsis grandiflora* varies between red and orange. Self-clinging deciduous campsis are excellent for covering a warm wall.

THE TRUMPET VINES

Campsis – the showy trumpet vines – are excellent for covering large walls and fences. They are deciduous and quite hardy, but need a sunny position to ripen the wood to produce their orange trumpets in summer. They can be cut hard back in winter and will produce long shoots in early summer which soon attach themselves to a support by aerial roots.

• *Campsis × tagliabuana* 'Madame Galen' Has wide-mouthed, orange-red, trumpet flowers.

• *C. radicans flava* Has yellow trumpet flowers.

• *C. grandiflora* Deep orange or red trumpets that are yellow inside.

PLANTS FOR DRY SHADE

As mentioned on page 30, many ivies will do well in dry shade. Use a plain green ivy for a wall that fades into the background or a large leaved variegated ivy like *Hedera colchica* 'Sulphur Heart', to create a more dramatic back–drop.

Euonymus fortunei cultivars are best known as garden shrubs, with their glossy evergreen leaves, usually brightly coloured in shades of green, lime, cream and yellow. The less well–known *Euonymus fortunei radicans* will develop roots against a wall and scramble up it. These plants are useful as they will tolerate dry shade and are evergreen. Like ivy, they can be used where few other plants will grow (see page 58).

DENSE GREEN COVER

If you want to turn your house completely green, Boston ivy (*Parthenocissus triscuspidata*) is the climber you need. The leaves of this vigorous plant are oval and have three lobes. The Boston ivy has splendid autumn colour and withstands a certain amount of drought. *P.t.* 'Lowii' has smaller, toothed leaves. *Parthenocissus henryana* has wonderfully subtle colouring, with velvety green leaves with silver veins and dark red undersides. In autumn it becomes deep scarlet. This plant is particularly good for shady walls.

GARDEN KNOW-HOW

Covering a fence

The evergreen honeysuckles *Lonicera japonica* 'Halliana', and the closely related 'Hall's Prolific', are fast-growing plants that will cover an unattractive fence quickly. For covering a chain-link fence in record time, these deliciously scented yellow- and white-flowered Japanese honeysuckles cannot be bettered. The small tubular flowers appear in pairs in the leaf axils from mid-summer to autumn. If you are in a great hurry, buy one plant for every 60cm (24in) of fence. Otherwise, space the plants out one to every 1m (3ft) or even more. They are best planted in the spring.

1 Prepare the ground thoroughly as described on page 10.

2 Plant the honeysuckles, firming them well in. The planting holes can be smaller than for many climbers, 20 x 20cm (8 x 8in) is sufficient, unless you buy plants that are growing in large pots and have a larger root ball.

3 Thread the growing tips of the twining stems through the wire but leave one or two of them to grow along the ground where they will soon root. You can help this process by placing small stones along the shoot so that it remains in contact with the ground.

4 When the shoots root themselves into the soil, which they do intermittently along their length, you can snip through the stems between each rooted section and each section will become a new plant.

5 Every four to five years the honeysuckle can be clipped hard back after flowering to form a dense screen.

CARING FOR HONEYSUCKLE

Honeysuckles are very easy to grow and need little attention except for tidying up. Mulch lightly with leaf-mould or well-rotted compost, every year in spring.

ROSES FOR WALLS

Climbing roses are a classic choice for house walls, closely followed by clematis. They will need training on horizontal wires or trellis. When choosing a colour, remember that strong pinks and reds do not always look their best against some bricks.

• *R.* 'Madame Alfred Carrière' is frequently recommended for shady walls; the colour, white with a pink tinge, shows up well and it is tolerant of most soils and conditions. This is a long-flowering rose, starting in summer and continuing through to autumn.

• *R.* 'Mermaid' is a single, yellow rose that will flower on a north wall.

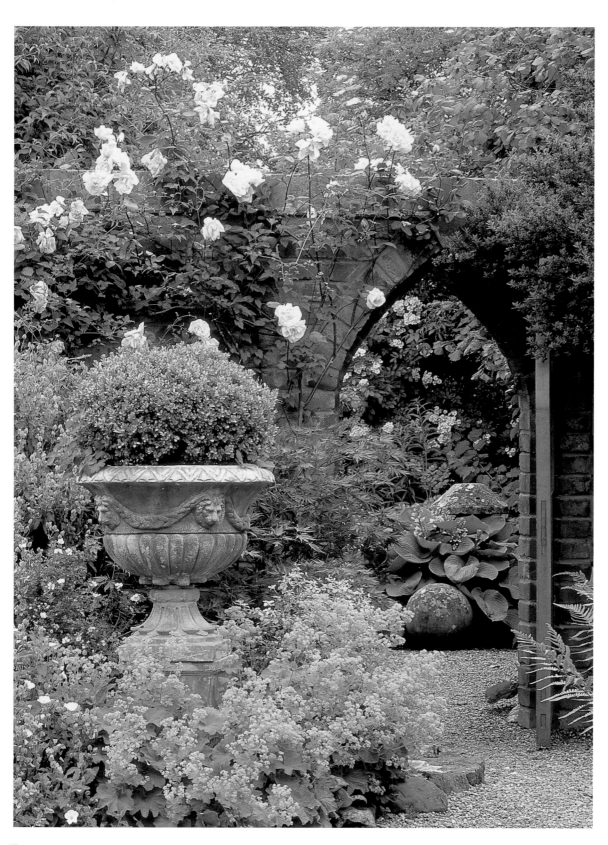

The soft yellow flowers of the old tea rose, *R.* 'Climbing Lady Hillingdon' show up to perfection on this old brick garden wall. 'Lady Hillingdon' needs a warm, protected wall to flower well and if happy, will flower from summer until mid-winter.

• Other roses that are often used on a shady wall success-fully are *R.* 'Madame Grégoire Staechlin', a pretty bright pink; the once-flowering mauve *R.* 'Veilchenblau'; and blush pink 'New Dawn'.

• If you have a sunny wall, choose the rambling Banksian rose (*R. banksiae* var. *banksiae*) which is white. There is also a yellow version (*R.b.* 'Lutea'). It is vigorous, thornless and has delicious clusters of frilly rosette flowers in May.

• *R.* 'Climbing Lady Hillingdon' has warm yellow-apricot flowers and a wonderful spicy scent and is also perfect for a warm wall.

SHRUB ROSES FOR WALLS OR PILLARS

Shrub roses can sometimes be trained against walls, even though they are not climbers. The Penzance briars like, 'Meg Merrilees' and 'Lady Penzance' can be used to clothe a tripod. Bourbon roses such as 'Louise Odier', 'Reine Victoria', 'Madame Pierre Oger' and 'Madame Ernest Calvat' are shrub roses, but all of them will do well on pergolas, tripods and trellis with the required support. Think twice about training Bourbon roses against walls as they may succumb to mildew and blackspot due to reduced airflow around their stems. 'Madame Pierre Oger' is a beautiful rose with double pink flowers, but it is particularly prone to these diseases.

"English" roses originate from crosses between the old-fashioned roses and modern varieties. They have been bred to combine the best features of each: the flowers are cup shaped or rosettes like the old varieties with many small petals and a rich fragrance, but the colour range is wider and they have more than one flush of flowers each year, charac-teristics they inherit from modern rose varieties. The taller English roses make excellent climbers for the small garden, as many grow to 1.8–2.4m (6–8ft). 'A Shropshire Lad' is a soft, peachy pink; 'Falstaff' is dark crimson; 'Graham Thomas' is a rich yellow, while 'Snow Goose' has white pompom–like flowers. 'Shropshire Lass' is a delicate flesh pink, while 'Constance Spry' has large pink flowers, but blooms only once each year.

CHOICE CLEMATIS

• Some of the large-flowered clematis, such as 'Nelly Moser', 'Lasurstern', 'Gipsy Queen' and 'Hagley Hybrid' may fade in hot sun and are best placed on walls that are shaded in the hottest part of the day.

• For sunny, sheltered walls, winter–flowering evergreen clematis are ideal. Try the large-leaved *C. armandii* with white,

OTHER SUITABLE CLIMBERS

• Wisteria has long racemes of pea flowers in white or mauve, varying from 10–15cm (6–8in) long in *W. brachybotrys* and its cultivars, to 1–1.2 m. (3–4ft) in the Japanese wisterias (*W. floribunda cvs*).

• *Actinidia kolomikta* has slightly heart-shaped leaves, green but turning white with a pink flush in sunshine. The flowers are insignif-icant but the foliage is striking.

• *Ampelopsis megalophylla* has huge leaves and black berrries, and *Ampelopsis glandulosa brevipedunculata* has bright blue berries and shows up well against house walls.

• Take advantage of the warmth of south-facing walls to try semi-tender climbers like *Solanum jasminoides* 'Album', *Campsis tagliabuana* 'Madame Galen', the star jasmine (*Trachelospermum jasminoides*) or the passion flower (*Passiflora caerulea*).

sweetly scented flowers from early spring, *C.a.* 'Apple Blossom' which has pink buds which open to white or *C.a.* 'Snowdrift' which has larger white flowers.

• In contrast, the leaves of *Clematis cirrhosa* are finely cut. *C.c. balearica* has cream bells speckled with brown. *C.c.* 'Wisley Cream' has creamy primrose bells and *C.c.* 'Freckles' has creamy-pink bells with red speckles.

PLANTING CLIMBERS AGAINST WALLS

When planting against a wall, remember to prepare the ground at the foot thoroughly, as the soil is liable to dry out. Follow the instructions for preparing dry ground for planting on page 10.

The terrace or the border in front of the wall can be wide and well planted, using the wall simply as a background. Alternatively, the wall planted with climbing plants can dominate the scene and any border at the foot should be narrow and modest. An ordinary brick wall can be thickly planted with varieties of roses, for example and have a simple line of lavender at the foot. An old stone wall might be better left almost bare as a restful background for a much wider, thickly planted border.

Trellis

TRELLIS CAN BE USED IN MANY DIFFERENT WAYS – to divide the garden up and create enclosed areas or to form arbours, summerhouses, pillars and obelisks. It is also frequently found as a simple support for climbing plants – attached to a wall, topping a wooden fence or as a free-standing screen. It is a versatile material which can be stained or painted in a variety of colours, but avoid overusing it in a garden or it will detract from the plants.

ON A WALL

Trellis is often attached to a wall to support twining climbers, where it creates a geometric pattern across the surface. It is this pleasing geometry that makes trellis a good supporter of a wide variety of climbing plants. Leaves and flowers with their rounded forms and twining stems contrast with it beautifully. It does need to be fixed carefully about 2.5cm (1in) away from the wall to allow air circulation and room for the plants to be fixed on or twined through (for more information on this see page 13).

AS A DIVIDER

Trellis is a relatively cheap and easy way of dividing a garden, adding height and visual interest. It makes an attractive, lightweight barrier which allows light and air through – good for plants which are prone to mildew – and at close quarters you can see through it and glimpse areas of the garden beyond. It is perfect for the ornamental areas of the garden, but could also be used to support runner beans and turn a vegetable garden into an enclosed and ornamental potager.

Clematis montana makes a breathtaking sight in late spring, flowering luxuriantly and with unfailing regularity. This plant is getting slightly top-heavy for the trellis and will need cutting back immediately after flowering.

TYPES OF TRELLIS

Trellis panels come in many different designs, some with a diagonal pattern, others square, some with a smaller mesh and others larger. There are panels with curved tops or even panels with *trompe l'oeil* patterns such as a series of diminishing arches that create a false perspective. Avoid very cheap trellis, as you may find that just as the climbing plants become mature, the trellis will begin to fall apart. Always choose trellis which has been pressure-treated with wood preservative.

SURFACE TREATMENTS

• If you leave the trellis in its natural colour, it will go silvery in time and blends very pleasantly with any plant fixed to it.

• Painted white trellis is readily available but white has its disadvantages in the garden. When new, it "jumps forward" and grabs your attention and as it gets older, it gets dirty and stained with lichen.

• Trellis can also be bought ready treated with a green wood preservative, which creates a subtle effect and goes well in most situations.

• There is a huge variety of brightly coloured wood stains on the market and it is very tempting to play about with colour and add dramatic effects yourself. You need to be careful however, and choose colours that do not detract or clash with the plants. In cooler climates where the light levels are low, a dark blue–grey is good with rich red roses. A very dark green is a safe colour, as are pale tones of ochre and terracotta.

Roses, red 'Galway Bay' and pink 'Clair Matin', and a yellow honeysuckle make a not-quite impenetrable screen behind a border.

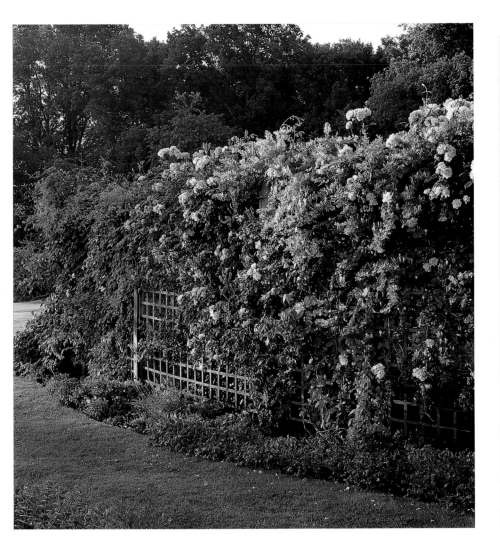

PLANTS FOR TRELLIS

• The honeysuckle *Lonicera similis* var. *delavayi*, which is not too vigorous, has a strong perfume and is reputed never to get aphids.

• Miniature climbing roses, such as *R* 'Chewpixel' (Open Arms), *R* 'Chewizz' (Warm Welcome).

• "English" roses, such as 'Crown Princess Margareta' which is a bright apricot-orange; 'Gertrude Jekyll', rich pink; and 'Tess of the D'Ubervilles' which is bright crimson.

• *Mauryandya barclayana*, with pinky-purple snapdragon flowers.

• *Lophospermum scandens*, which has a range of pink, purple, white and lavender flowers (often called *Asarina*).

• *Apios americana*, an unusual twining plant for a shady position. It is very hardy and flowers in late summer, early autumn, with clusters of pea-shaped flowers variously described as maroon, chocolate or blood-red.

• *Kadsura japonica*, an unusual evergreen twiner which has pale yellow flowers followed by round fruits which resemble globes of scarlet berries. It is best in semi-shade but needs a warm, sheltered spot and acid soil.

COLOUR SCHEMES

If the wall is painted and will need repainting in the future, then the trellis can be hinged, allowing it to be leant forwards and moved away from the wall without damaging the plants.

When painting or repainting a wall, think twice before using white masonry paint. As mentioned above, white tends to "jump out", shows every mark and then tends to develop moulds. Cream, pale sand, palest grey and pale pink, all reflect the light well and are good backgrounds for many flowers. Rich colours like dark blue, green and red are exciting with pale flowers growing against them. If the climbers you hope to grow have flowers that contrast with the wall colour, it is better to paint any trellis in a toning shade, perhaps a little darker than the wall. The overall effect should not be too fussy.

Climbers as ground cover

CLIMBING PLANTS do not have to be grown up vertical surfaces. Some will grow happily along the ground and make dense and effective ground cover in difficult places. In fact, some plants even flower better when the stems are horizontal.

PLANTS TO TRY

• Among the best are the ivies. Some of the larger-leaved ivies make excellent ground cover where nothing else will grow, such as in dry shade under trees. Try *Hedera canariensis* 'Ravensholst', *H. colchica* 'Dentata', *H. helix* var. *baltica* and *H.h.* 'Green Ripple'.

• *Euonymus fortunei radicans* with its glossy, deep green oval leaves and the broad-leaved Irish ivy, *H. Hibernica* will do well in dry shady conditions.

• Several members of the rubus family, which also contains blackberries and raspberries, make a good ground cover when they have nothing to scramble up. *Rubus ichangensis* has panicles of white flowers, followed by edible fruits and semi-evergreen, glossy, tapered heart-shaped leaves. *R. irenaeus* has round leaves, up to 15cm (6in) across, with a wavy edge, small white flowers in summer followed by large red fruits. *R. lineatus* has a silvery sheen on the undersides of the leaves and distinctive parallel veins. *R. flagelliflorus* is graceful, with white-felted stems and shiny black fruits.

This shady corner in a town garden is stylish and almost maintenance free. The stone urn is surrounded by climbers grown as ground cover for all-year effect. Tough, adaptable *Euonymus fortunei* 'Emerald 'n' Gold' which will climb in the right circumstances, adds light and sparkle and contrasts with the large glossy leaves of the ivy.

• Everlasting pea (*Lathyrus latifolius*) can be allowed to sprawl over the ground. Unlike the annual sweet pea, the racemes of pinky–purple flowers do not have to be picked regularly and they continue until autumn.

• *Anredera cordifolia* has highly fragrant racemes of white flowers in autumn and, although slightly tender, will re-grow from the base in cooler climates. Alternatively, lift and store the tuberous roots like dahlias.

• Wood vamp (*Decumaria barbara*), a climbing hydrangea with white flower clusters and glossy oval leaves, is also good for ground cover.

• Clematis too flower well when grown horizontally and can be grown with another ground cover plant.

TRAINING ROSES

Training the shoots of climbing and rambling roses horizontally makes them flower right along their length instead of just at the tips. Some roses can be pegged right down to the ground to produce blooms at a low level. Long growths should be pegged to the ground in late summer. Any side shoots should be cut back to about 10cm (4in). The following season these will flower, making a pleasing mound covered in bloom. Try this with the following roses; 'Kathleen Harrop', 'Zéphirine Drouhin', and 'Martha', which are all thornless, or 'Blairii No. 2'.

Planting ivy as ground cover

Ivy, *Hedera sp.* and *cvs*, makes a good ground cover as it is tough, hardy and evergreen. Requiring an almost neutral or alkaline soil, it roots as it goes and, after a slow start, will make a dense covering. There are many different types and although variegations may not be as good in shade, if there is some sun, white, cream or yellow variegated types can be used to create a rich tapestry.

1 The ground should be free from weeds, particularly perennial weeds like dandelion, docks, nettles and ground elder. Dig these out carefully (A), or use a herbicide, following the manufacturer's instructions. If there is time, the ground can be covered with black plastic or old carpet for a season to smother the weeds (B).

2 Dig in some well rotted manure, dried chicken manure or compost (C).

3 Plant the ivy plants at about 45cm (18in) apart (D). The ivy can be trimmed over in subsequent years to keep it tidy.

ALTERNATIVE METHOD
Cover the ground with black sheet mulch. In early autumn, take hardwood cuttings from an established ivy plant. They should be 15–20cm (6–8in long) with the lower leaves removed. Make holes through the sheet and insert the cuttings so that one third of the length remains above the ground. These should be planted much closer together, say at 25cm (10in) apart. This method saves weeding. In the first method, the ground will need to be kept clear of weeds until the plants have formed a dense cover.

CLASSIC COMBINATIONS

*I*n the wild, climbing plants grow over trees and shrubs. Growing climbing plants like this enables you to get twice as many plants in the garden and extend the season of interest. In even the smallest garden there will be room for several clematis to scramble through the plants that are already there. In large gardens, trees that settle down to a dull middle age and an unexciting autumn can be enlivened by growing a vigorous climbing rose or Virginia creeper into them. The Roman poet Horace noticed that the 'beauteous marriageable vine' sometimes 'to the lusty Bridegroom Elm does Joyne'. So many climbing plants have been introduced from continent to continent since then that there are wonderful combinations to try wherever you may be.

Clematis 'Perle d'Azur' scrambles over the evergreen Shrubby hare's ear, *Bupleurum fruticosum*. The bupleurum has small yellow flowers in clusters from mid-summer to early autumn and is an ideal companion for the not too vigorous and particularly blue clematis.

Vigorous climbers for large trees

Vigorous climbers and large trees are a hungry combination and to ensure success, be prepared to take some trouble with the planting of the climber, which is, after all, an interloper. Observe it at regular intervals for the first two years or so, until it is well established; it may need a boost now and then, perhaps with a foliar feed.

PLANTING AGAINST A TREE

Plants that will grow up or into trees should be planted either right at the base of the tree where there are very few feeding roots or several metres (yards) beyond the edge of the tree's canopy where the feeding roots diminish. To plant a climber to grow into an ash or sycamore, it is better to plant the climber beyond the canopy. Support the climber on canes or strings until it reaches the lower branches. Oak trees have deeper roots, as do cherry and apple trees, and the climber will do better if planted close to the trunk. To ensure success, dig a large hole, line the sides with plastic sheeting and fill it with soil well enriched with organic matter.

VIGOROUS ROSES

The following roses are suitable to be grown into a tree:
• Himalayan musk rose (*Rosa brunonii*) has single white flowers in clusters and stems that grow to 5–12m (15–40ft) long. *R.b.* 'La Mortola' is an even stronger grower.
• *R. filipes* is hardier and has clusters of a hundred or more small creamy white flowers. The flower clusters on *R.f.* 'Kiftsgate' are even larger.
• White roses such as 'Bobbie James', 'Wedding Day', 'Rambling Rector' 'Toby Tristram' and *R. mulligani*.
• 'Paul's Himalayan Musk' is a soft pink.
• 'Easlea's Golden Rambler' is a rich yellow, as is 'Lawrence Johnson'.
• 'Desprez à Fleurs Jaunes' and 'Treasure Trove' are soft peachy-pink with yellow tones as well.
• 'Excelsa' is a light crimson.

FOLIAGE CLIMBERS

The Virginia creeper (*Parthenocissus quinquefolia*) is one of the easiest and most successful climbers to grow into a tree. Very hardy, it attaches itself by adhesive pads on its tendrils. The leaves are in groups of five, like the fingers of a hand and turn a glorious red in the autumn. *Parthenocissus tricuspidata*, the Boston Ivy, is another self-clinging vigorous vine that colours spectacularly in autumn.

Vitis coignetiae is the most dramatic of the ornamental vines, reaching 20m (60ft) into a tree and then flowing down. The large leaves turn red in the autumn. Other vines that can be encouraged to grow up through trees are *Vitis labrusca*, which will grow to 8–10m (24–30ft) and is very hardy, *V. davidii* and *V. amurensis*.

CLEMATIS FOR TREES

Clematis grow over trees in the wild and they really thrive when grown like this.
• *Clematis terniflora* is a very vigorous species and has white scented bell flowers between late summer and mid-autumn. This would make a good partner to a spring-flowering *C. montana* cultivar, like *C.m. grandiflora* over a large tree.

Clematis montana and a climbing rose were planted to mingle above this window but the clematis much prefers the laburnum.

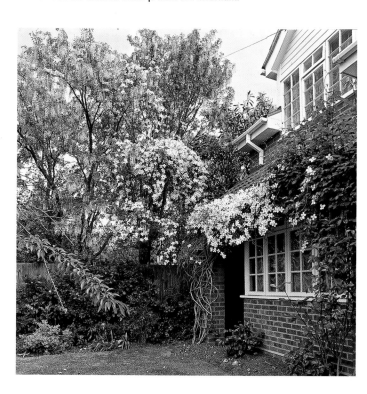

• *C. × vedrariensis* 'Rosea' is similar to *C.m.* 'Rubens', the pink flowered montana, but the leaves bear some of the pale hairs associated with one of its parents, *C. chrysocoma*. The variety 'Hidcote' has small, deeper pink flowers. All of these will grow to 7–10m (21–30ft) in height.

• *Clematis flammula*, with white, star-shaped flowers from late summer to mid-autumn is another late bloomer that is good through trees.

• *C. armandii* has handsome elliptical leaves and white scented flowers very early in the year.

• For warmer gardens, the winter-flowering *C. cirrhosa* will climb to 4m (12ft).

OTHER VIGOROUS PLANTS

The American bittersweet, *Celastrus scandens*, is a deciduous, twining plant with pale yellow flowers which are followed by yellow berries in red-lined seed cases. *C. orbiculatus*, the Oriental bittersweet, is similar, but the flowers are pale green and it is more vigorous. To get the berries you need to buy the hermaphrodite form and it will take about three years to settle in. The leaves of both turn yellow in autumn but *C. scandens* is more tolerant about position and drought. Both vines will need encouraging into the tree initially.

The long clusters of purple or white flowers of the wisterias look magnificent tumbling down from the canopy of a tall tree. Climbing hydrangeas and schizophragmas with their large white flower heads are also splendid.

Less common climbers for trees

• *Actinidia arguta*, from the same genus as the kiwi fruit, will grow to 20m (60ft) in a tree. It is very hardy and has small white fragrant flowers in summer, followed, if two plants are grown, by edible oval fruits. These are not as well flavoured as the kiwi fruits that are sold commercially. *A. melanandra* has small lance-shaped leaves with blue-white undersides on pink stalks and white flowers.

• *Akebia quinata*, the chocolate vine, is very fast growing and can be invasive. It has attractive foliage and vanilla-scented, chocolate-coloured flowers.

• *Tripterygium regalii* grows to about 6m (18ft). It is an unusual climber with handsome oval leaves about 15cm (6in) long. In late summer, panicles of small white flowers are followed by greenish fruits with three wings.

The climbing hydrangea, *Hydrangea petiolaris*, will as happily hoist itself into a tree as it will cling to a wall, but in both cases, it will need encouragement to do so for the first year or two.

APPLE TREES

Gardeners lucky enough to have an orchard full of elderly apple trees can use these as supports for the less vigorous climbing and rambling roses, or taller old roses. Noisette roses and those derived from *R. wichurana* look beautiful grown in this way and come into flower after the apple blossom has fallen and before the fruit itself makes a decorative contribution to the garden. Suitable roses include *R.* 'Climbing Cécile Brunner', 'Alister Stella Gray', 'Evangeline', 'Dr W. Van Fleet' and 'Champney's Pink Cluster'.

Climbers for scrambling over shrubs and hedges

COUNTRY HEDGEROWS USED TO HOST A TANGLE OF CLIMBERS – bryony, honeysuckle, Old Man's Beard, roses – and were beautiful to look at all year. Scrambling through shrubs and small trees is the natural way for many slender climbers to grow. In nature the plants put themselves where they want to be, often germinating in deep shade and finding their way to the sunny side of the shrub. They grow without any attention.

PLANTING

Dig a planting hole, as described on page 10, at the outer edge of the shrub's canopy on the windward side. You want the wind to blow the climber towards the shrub and not away from it. It need not be quite as large as 30 x 30cm (12 x 12in) if the roots of the shrub are in the way. As with all other plants, make sure that the plant is thoroughly watered on a regular basis.

PLANTS FOR DAPPLED SHADE

• *Codonopsis convolvulacea* is very good for scrambling through and over shrubs in the woodland garden. It has bell-shaped, light blue flowers and it likes dappled shade, as do *C. affinis*, with purple green bells and *C. lanceolata* which is larger and has green-purple bells with purple flecks inside. The codonopsis flower in late summer and are ideal for adding interest to early summer flowering shrubs like deutzia, chaenomeles and azaleas.

• The climbing monkshood, *Aconitum hemsleyanum*, can be grown easily from seed but it is better to buy a guaranteed dark blue plant from a nursery, as some seed-grown plants can often be an insipid mauve. It flowers usefully late from mid-summer until autumn and the flowers go well with late-flowering shrubs such as escallonia or with the red berries of a cotoneaster or the fruits of a berberis.

• The climbing fumitory, *Adlumia fungosa*, has fern-like leaves and drooping pinky-white flowers similar to those of a dicentra. Grow it from seed and plant out as soon as there are about six leaves. Grow it up a trained wall shrub such as pyracantha or chaenomeles.

• *Dicentra scandens* has bunches of pendent, yellow, slightly heart-shaped flowers, tipped with pink or light purple and light, ferny foliage. It will twine through shrubs and can be cut back after the frosts. *D. macrocapnos* has similar flowers but is more vigorous.

• *Paederia scandens* is a hardy deciduous twiner with dark green leaves. Large panicles of small creamy tubular flowers with purple throats appear late in the year. *P. foetida* has lilac flowers and *P. tomentosa* has rose-purple flowers.

• The flame vine, *Tropaeolum speciosum*, flourishes in places with cool damp summers and moist soil. It is often seen growing over yew hedges which show off the vivid red flowers to perfection. The flowers are followed by deep blue fruits contrasting with purplish bracts. *T. azureum* is smaller, with blue flowers. *T. tuberosum* (of which the most widely available form is *T.t. lineamaculatum* 'Ken Aslet') has blue-green leaves and long-spurred, orange-red flowers. *T. tricolorum* which grows to about 1.2m (4ft) is for warmer climates only and has striking orange or yellow flowers from red-orange, black-tipped calyces (the outer protective part of the flower consisting of fused sepals which form a tube).

PLANTS FOR SUN

• *Billardiera longiflora* has long, lime-yellow flowers in later summer, followed by vivid violet-blue berries. It needs wall protection and full sun or can be grown in a container and taken inside in the winter.

• *Dichelostemma volubile* is a half-hardy perennial that grows from a swollen root. The allium-like leaves can be 60cm (24in) long and the flowering stem over 1m (3ft). The stem twines through its host shrub so that the pink flowers are in the sun. A shrub border against a south wall would suit it but it still needs protecting against frost.

• Moonseed, *Menispermum canadense*, has large round leaves on long stalks. The flowers are an inconspicuous greenish–white and are followed by small black fruits.

• The Chilean glory flower, *Eccremocarpus scaber*, with orange, red or yellow flowers, is an annual or short–lived perennial climber that will scramble over small shrubs.

Most of these climbers die back at the end of the year and can be tidied up then. The Eccremocarpus dies back to a small tuber and can be either dug up like a dahlia or mulched. The Billardiera can be planted out in a pot which is sunk into the ground. This can then be brought into a frost–free place during the winter.

The vivid red flowers and pretty five-lobed leaves of *Tropaeolum speciosum*, the flame creeper from Chile show up beautifully against dark yew, *Taxus baccata*.

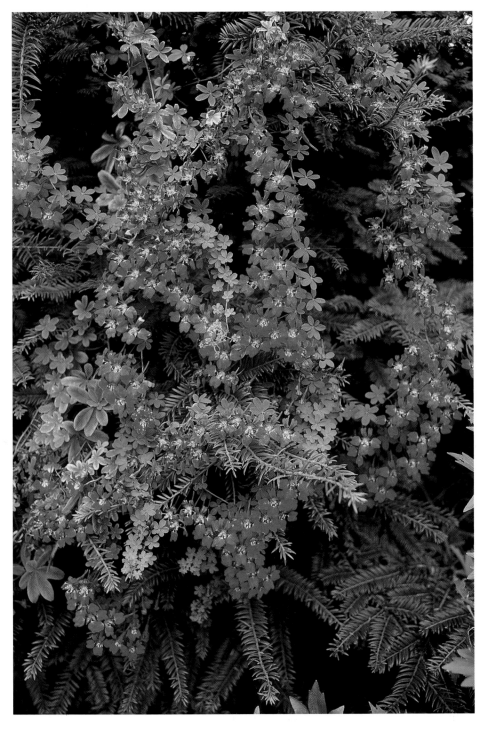

A LIVING SUPPORT

Using one climber to support another is a good way of extending the season of interest throughout the year. Vines, *Vitis* species, are useful for this. They are fast growing and soon produce a woody framework capable of supporting some of the less vigorous flowering climbers. Ornamental vines are often at their best in late summer and autumn, when they are fruiting and the leaves colour, so make good companions for early-flowering climbers like *Clematis alpina* and *C. macropetala*. Suitable species are *Vitis davidii, V. riparia, V. thunbergii* and *V. labrusca. V parvifolia* is particularly charming, with copper-coloured new foliage and small but profuse glossy green-bronze leaves in summer. Its rich autumn colour is accompanied by tiny blue-tinged black fruits. Do not try to grow anything over fruiting grapevines as these need all the air and sunshine they can get.

All pruning should be carried out in winter before the sap rises. Train the vine to form a permanent framework and cut back to one or two buds to form a spur system which becomes more attractive with age. Excessive growth should be stopped at five to six leaves in mid-summer and this often means that there are leaves of different ages which is a pleasant contrast. The support systems need to be very sturdy for a vine, and tall enough as vines grow quickly in the season (see pages 70–73 for detailed information on training and caring for vines).

Clematis couples

CLEMATIS ARE VERY "LIGHT" CLIMBERS and can be trained with and over many other plants, such as honeysuckle, roses, vines or climbing hydrangea, without damaging them. They can be grown in pairs and even the smallest garden has room for one or even two more. They need careful planting to give their best and pruning can be complicated (see pages 20–21).

COMBINING CLEMATIS

If you plan to plant your clematis in pairs, then it will save trouble if you choose two plants that both need the same pruning regime. You can mix two late, large-flowering hybrids like purple-red 'Ernest Markham' and white 'Huldine' which both need lots of sun to flower well or the blue 'Perle d'Azur' with shell pink 'Hagley Hybrid', both of which will take more shade.

For a late-flowering combination in a sunny position, 'Madame Baron Veillard' is a bright lilac-pink and would combine well with a viticella cultivar like 'Venosa Violacea'. Two early flowering clematis which would look well together are C. alpina 'Helsingborg' which is deep purple and C.a. 'Ruby' which is a soft red. Neither of these need pruning.

When planting, make the planting hole (see page 10) twice as deep rather than twice as wide and add a thick layer of well-rotted organic matter at the base as you will be feeding two plants. Make sure that the surface of the root-balls are at least 7.5 cm (3in) and preferably nearer 15cm (6in) below soil level.

CLEMATIS WITH OTHER CLIMBERS

Clematis can be grown with other climbers, too.
• The purple leaves of Vitis vinifera 'Purpurea' look sumptuous with Clematis 'Etoile Violette' or 'Ernest Markham'.
• Silver or white variegated ivies form a good background for shade-tolerant, mid-blue C. 'William Kennett' and bright pink C. 'Scartho Gem' which has a deeper bar.
• Another good combination for shade is the climbing hydrangea (Hydrangea anomala petiolaris) with rosy-lilac C. 'Comtesse de Bouchaud'.
• C. 'Gravetye Beauty' has ruby-red flowers until mid-autumn which show up well against silver-leaved shrubs.
• Other good contrasts are yellow C. 'Bill Mackenzie' with the late-flowering perennial pea Lathyrus latifolius or the golden hop, Humulus lupulus 'Aureus'.

• C. tangutica with the climbing monkshood, Aconitum hemsleyanum which is blue.
• Rose 'Golden Showers' with violet-purple C. 'Etoile Violette'.
• Rose crimson C. 'Kermesina' or the large lavender-blue flowers of C. 'Lasurstern' are very pretty against yellow variegated ivies such as Hedera helix 'Oro di Bogliasco'.
• The self-clinging Virginia creeper (Parthenocissus quinquefolia) will support any of the clematis and provide a handsome backdrop of foliage.

CLEMATIS WITH SHRUBS

Woody wall shrubs like the Japanese quince (Chaenomeles) or wall-trained pyracanthas are perfect hosts for clematis. Choose clematis that flower at different times to their host shrubs to extend the season of interest. The Japanese quince flowers early on old wood and can be kept trimmed back, allowing the clematis to display its flowers well. Use the quince as a host for summer-flowering, large-flowered clematis. You could even increase the succession of flowers against the wall by adding a late-flowering C. viticella cultivar.

CONTRASTING SHAPES

Contrasting colours are very eye-catching, but a contrast of shapes in similar colours also works very well. There are many possibilities:
• Clematis montana and Rosa 'Sombreuil'.
• Rosa 'Climbing Iceberg' with the pretty small-flowered C. × triternata 'Rubromarginata' which has rosy red edges to the petals.
• Blue wisteria with C. 'Perle d'Azur'.
• White Wisteria sinensis and Clematis montana. They are both very hardy and vigorous.

These pictures show the different effects that can be created when the same clematis is paired with different plants. The picture above shows *Clematis* 'Perle d'Azur' paired with *Rosa* 'Morning Jewel', this coupling is very harmonious; the image on the right shows the vibrant blue of the clematis contrasting with golden hop *Humulus lupulus* and *Lonicera* 'Graham Thomas'.

COMPARING COLOURS

Most container-grown clematis will be in flower when you see them in the garden centre or nursery. It is easy to check colour combinations by doing what Vita Sackville West used to do at Sissinghurst. Carry the plant round and put it beside its prospective companion to see how it looks. Even if one climber is supposed to come into flower just as another has gone over, this does not always go to plan so it is as well if the colours pleasantly enhance each other.

EDIBLES

*C*limbing plants that produce edible fruits or vegetables fit well into the kitchen garden, turning a utilitarian vegetable plot into an ornamental potager. When properly supported, both annual and perennial climbers can be used to create enclosures, provide shelter from wind and create light shade as well as being decorative and fruitful.

Annual fruits and vegetables, such as squashes and runner beans, add instant height to flower beds, and form screens very quickly. They can have a different position in the garden every year. Others, like vines and brambles, are more permanent features in the productive garden.

The chestnut fence surrounding a vegetable plot makes a good support for pumpkin squash 'Baby Bear', combined with *Cobaea scandens*, the cup and saucer vine, a fast-growing climber usually grown as an annual.

Grapevines

THERE ARE MANY SPECIES OF VINE that are purely ornamental and these are referred to in other chapters. In this chapter, the emphasis is on the fruiting vine, *Vitis vinifera* and its cultivars and hybrids. Grapevines are adaptable plants and tougher than many people realize. You can grow them for their fruit as you see them in commercial vineyards, sometimes with only a short leg and one long stem on each side. In a sunny, sheltered vegetable garden, such vines make attractive edgings to the beds.

Conversely, you can grow a grapevine as an ornamental, enjoying its attractive leaves. Vines in Mediterranean countries are often used as shade providers, trained over pergolas and arbours. They still produce fruit, the long bunches of grapes hanging down invitingly from the roof, but not so intensively. In cooler climates, many varieties need to be grown against a warm, sunny wall or under glass to produce edible fruit, but not all. Many vines are quite hardy, especially those derived from the American *V. labrusca*.

PLANTING

Grapes must have a sheltered, sunny site. Choose the site carefully, prepare the ground and ensure good drainage by adding gravel or sand to the enriched soil (see pages 10–11). On very acid soil, add lime; on a poor soil add plenty of well-rotted garden compost.

Year-old vines should be planted in the winter, 1.2–1.5m (4–5ft) apart. If you are planting a single vine against a wall, position it 23cm (9in) from the wall. Each plant will need a vertical cane or post as a support. Spread the roots out well, then fill the hole with soil and firm in well. Prune the vine down to two good buds from ground level. In early spring, apply a general fertilizer and then mulch each plant with well-rotted compost.

SUPPORTING THE VINES

Grapes need supporting on wires, whether they are grown in the open or against a wall, and the wires need putting in place before the vines are planted. In the open, erect 2m (6ft) wooden posts, about 2.5m (8ft) apart, sinking them 60cm (24in) into the ground. Metal post supports are also ideal for this purpose, as they can be hammered into the ground and the posts bolted into them. Stretch three horizontal wires at 30cm (1ft) intervals between the posts, with the lowest 45cm (18in) above the ground. Fix the wires securely in place with staples. Plant the vines at least 2.5m (8ft) apart.

The grapevine growing over this barn is allowed to do its own thing and is more decorative than fruitful.

GRAPES FOR WALLS
- *V.* 'Himrod' is a seedless variety of golden grape.
- *V.* 'Triomphe d'Alsace' is a black grape suitable for dessert or wine.
- *V.* 'Léon Millot' has black grapes and is very reliable. Its vigour makes it a good decorative vine to grow against a wall.
- *V.v.* 'Chasselas' has white, well-flavoured fruit and must be grown on a warm wall.
- The strawberry grape, *V.* 'Fragola', has red fruits that smell of strawberries.

Training a grapevine

These instructions show how to train a grape-vine on wires to produce the maximum amount of fruit. If you do not want to embark on such a complicated regime and are just growing one grapevine against a wall or over a pergola, remember that grapevines produce their fruit on shoots growing from one-year-old stems. If the vine is not pruned and trained at all, it will soon become a tangle. Aim to produce a permanent woody framework that encourages the yearly production of new wood.

1 Plant the vine you have bought from a garden centre, nursery or specialist grower in the spring. Allow one shoot to develop during the summer and train it vertically up the post or cane. Pinch other shoots back to one leaf.

2 In late autumn, cut the vine down again to within 45cm (18in) of the ground, leaving just three buds (A).

3 The following spring, three shoots will grow and these should be trained vertically. If any side shoots appear, pinch them back to one leaf.

4 In autumn of that year, tie down one of the shoots to the left and another to the right, along the wires. Cut them back to about 75cm (30in) long. Cut the central stem back to three buds (B).

5 In the summer of the subsequent year, those three buds will grow into three new stems and these should be trained vertically. The horizontal stems will develop laterals that will grow vertically and bear fruit (C). In the first fruiting year, do not allow the vine to carry more than two or three bunches of grapes; during the next season, they can be allowed to bear four or five and after that they can bear a full crop.

6 In the autumn, these fruit-bearing horizontals must be pruned back and the vertical shoots from the centre will provide the replacements which should be pruned and tied in as before (D).

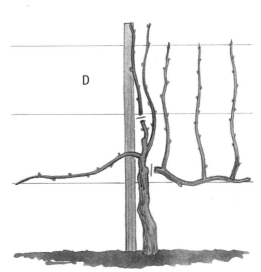

A standard grapevine

A standard grapevine does not take up too much room and can be grown either in the ground or in a pot which can be moved in and out of a greenhouse or conservatory. Grapevines need a cold period during the winter, but the fruit needs a long, warm ripening period and a container-grown vine makes this possible in many areas.

1 Take a year-old vine and plant it in an 18cm (7in) pot with some crocks at the base, filled with John Innes No. 3 compost. Alternatively, plant it in a prepared planting hole in the ground (see page 10). Choose the hottest site you can find but not one that is too sheltered, as grapes need air circulation. In late autumn, cut the main stem back to a bud about 15cm (6in) from the compost.

2 The following spring and summer, train the vine up a cane and pinch the side shoots back to one leaf (A).

3 Next winter, cut the stem back to a bud 90–150cm (3–5ft) above the compost, depending on the height you want your standard vine to be. Repot the plant into a 38cm (15in) pot and remove all the side shoots (B).

4 In the following summer, let four or five shoots develop from the top, but stop them when they have made five or six leaves. Still keep the stem clear and remove any flowers if necessary.

5 That winter, prune each of the four or five shoots back to one bud (C). Repot the vine again, this time into a 45cm (18in) pot. Keep the vine securely staked.

6 In the subsequent season, let the vine produce two bunches of grapes and pinch out the branches at two leaves beyond the fruit. The other laterals should be pinched back to five leaves and any sub-lateral shoots back to one leaf (D).

A

B

C

D

MAKING YOUR OWN PLANTS

If you already have a vine, prunings root very easily. These are cheap and fun to use for different growing methods. Take a 25–30cm (10–12in) hardwood pruning, trimmed above and below a bud and insert it into the ground to two thirds of its length in a sheltered spot in sandy soil in mid–autumn.

In this garden a vine has been used as an ornamental, trained attractively over an arch.

CARING FOR YOUR STANDARD VINE

The compost should never be allowed to dry out. Top dress the soil each winter by removing the top 2.5cm (1in) of soil in the container and replacing it with fresh compost. In the open ground, mulch round the base of the grapevine with compost or well–rotted manure. In the first year, apply a liquid feed every week until late summer. In subsequent years, do this until the fruit has set. You can help the flowers to fertilize themselves by shaking the vine gently when it is in bloom. Bunches of fruit may need thinning out.

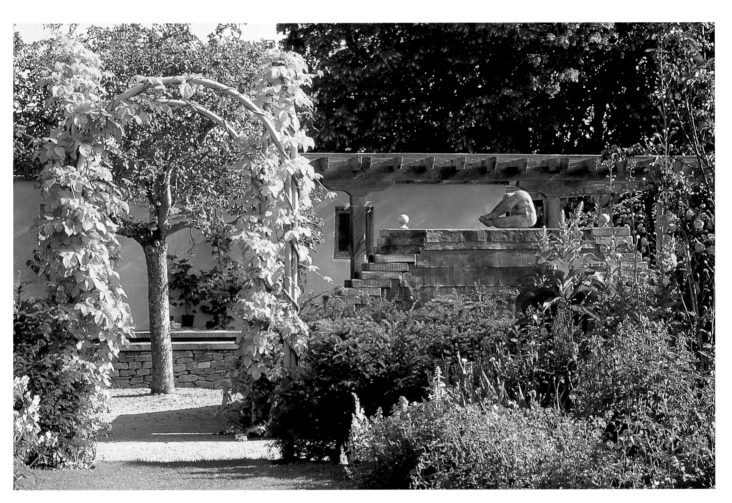

GRAPES FOR PERGOLAS, ARBOURS, ARCHES, POSTS AND WIRES

- *V.* 'Brant' has small bunches of black grapes and is particularly attractive when the leaves turn red in autumn.
- *V. labrusca* 'Concord' is a popular American grape.
- *V.* 'Boskoop Glory' is black, sweet and good for dessert.
- *V.* 'Cascade' (syn. V. Seibel 13053) is an early black grape, prolific and reliable.
- *V. vinifera* 'Incana' has leaves and stems covered in a fine grey-white down.
- *V. v.* 'Madeleine Angevine'.7672 is a dessert grape that is also used for wine.
- *V. v.* 'Siegerrebe' has golden berries and a muscat flavour.
- *V. v.* 'Madeleine Sylvaner 28/51' is a white grape for dessert and wine.
- *V. v.* 'Perlette' needs some thinning of its white seedless grapes as the bunches can get over-full of fruits.

Cane fruits

CLIMBING CANE FRUITS ARE very useful garden plants. Like ornamental climbers, the long stems they produce can be used on supports to give height in a garden, to grow through something else or to clothe a wall. Blackberries, loganberries, boysenberries, tayberries and other blackberry crosses are all useful and provide delicious fruit. There are other more unusual cane fruits, like the Japanese wineberry (*Rubus phoenicolasius*) that is particularly ornamental. The edible fruits are small, garnet-red and usually free from pests. The fruits of *Rubus flagelliflorus*, *R. setchuenensis*, *R. spectabilis* and *R. ichangensis* are edible although these canes are usually grown for their ornamental qualities.

PRUNING AND TRAINING CANE FRUITS

Most cane fruits can be trained against a trellis, a free-standing post or wire fencing (see 'A Blackberry Screen' opposite); or they can be left to naturally arch over.

1. Buy certificated virus-free plants. Plant them shallowly in a sunny, but not exposed, position. Blackberries fruit on one-year-old wood, so fruiting canes need to be kept separate from new canes. Train older canes to the lower wires and new ones to the higher, as in 'A Blackberry Screen' opposite.

2. At the end of winter, remove the old canes by cutting them down to the ground.

3. Pick up the new canes and tie them onto the wires, trellis or other support, leaving an equal distance between them.

4. The canes can be fanned out simply, or woven in any number of ways. See 'A Blackberry Screen' opposite.

CARING FOR CANE FRUITS

Plant the fruits 1.8–2.5m (6–8ft) apart, according to variety, in autumn. The following spring scatter a compound fertilizer at the amount suggested on the packet, in a 45cm (18in) diameter circle round each plant and rake it in lightly. Repeat this at the end of May and the end of June. In following years, mulch each spring with well-rotted manure.

Raspberry beetles, grey mould and birds may be problems. To prevent the problem of raspberry beetles, spray a derris-based insecticide at dusk when the blackberry flowers begin to open. For grey mould, keep plants clear of dead and dying material and provide good air circulation. If birds are especially troublesome, netting the plants is the answer.

CHOOSING PLANTS FOR A SCREEN

Plants with long, flexible canes are necessary and as there is much handling of the stems involved, thornless cultivars make the undertaking easier.

• *Rubus fruticosus laciniatus* 'Oregon Thornless' is slightly smaller than some other cultivars. Although it is a useful size for a medium garden, the stems are quite stout and need careful handling to weave them well.

• Other thornless varieties are: *R. fruticosus* 'Thornfree', *R.f.* 'Merton Thornless', and *R.f.* 'Waldo'.

• The hybrid *Rubus* 'Boysenberry, Thornless' is good on light soils and is very drought resistant and much less vigorous than blackberries.

• The fruits of loganberries can be up to 5cm (2in) long and *Rubus* (Loganberry Group) 'LY 654' is thornless.

• *Rubus phoenicolasius* (the Japanese wineberry) is very attractive and the red bristles on the stems are not too sharp to handle, although gloves are recommended.

The Japanese wineberry, *Rubus phoenicolasius*, has attractive fruits, stems covered with red hairs and pale green leaves, felted white on the underside.

A Blackberry Screen

Blackberry canes can be woven to make an attractive screen, from which it is much easier to pick the fruit than the usual tangled mass of stems. Loganberries, boysenberries and Japanese wineberries can also be trained in the same way.

1 Sink two 3m (9ft) posts firmly into the ground, 2.5m (8ft) apart, and stretch wires horizontally between them. Starting at about 1m (3ft) from the ground, you will need a wire every 30cm (12in).

2 Plant the canes between the two posts in winter, spacing them at 2.5m (8ft) intervals. Cut the plants back to a bud 25cm (10in) above the ground (A).

3 In early spring, fork some general fertilizer, such as pelleted chicken manure or blood, fish and bone, into the soil around the plants.

4 A month later, mulch the plant well with well-rotted garden compost, but do not let the compost touch the canes.

5 New canes will appear in summer and should be woven in and out of the wires (B).

6 In the following year, fruit will be carried on laterals of the previous year's canes. The new canes should be trained up through the centre of the bush and tied in to the top wire (C).

7 In autumn, after fruiting, all the fruited canes should be cut back to the base and the new canes are re-woven to take their place.

A

B

C

Cucurbits

THE CUCURBIT FAMILY CONTAINS many of the well-known climbing fruiting plants, including melons, cucumbers, marrows, pumpkins and squashes. These are all attractive plants with handsome large leaves and impressive and delicious fruits. They climb by means of tendrils, or will happily scramble over the ground and any obstacles they come across.

Also in this family are about 25 species of tropical and sub-tropical plants which are interesting and attractive to grow as well as being useful although inedible. In a warm climate or under glass, grow your own loofah, *Luffa cylindrica* or calabash, *Lagenaria vulgaris*.

GROWING CUCURBITS

Marrows, pumpkins and squashes are generally allowed to ramble over the ground because the fruits become so heavy. Some ornamental gourds and squashes, however, can be grown up wigwams or over pergolas and arches. They look splendid in a vegetable garden grown this way. Melons and cucumbers are generally grown as climbing plants. Against a wall, the fruits ripen better and they can be kept away from damp soil and pests more easily.

All these plants are grown as annuals in more or less the same way and they need good, rich moisture-retaining soil. Sow the seeds in pots in early spring. The temperature needs to be about 20°C (68°F) for them to germinate, so a heated propagator may be necessary. Plants can be moved outside in the middle of spring or grown on in a greenhouse border or growbags.

Cucumbers

Cucumber seeds need to be sown on their sides. Train the stems up canes and pinch out the growing point when the plant reaches the roof of the greenhouse. Pinch out the side shoots at two leaves beyond a female flower (one which has a small cucumber behind it). The plants need a moist atmosphere and regular feeding with a tomato fertilizer. Outdoor cucumbers can be left to scramble on the ground – protect the plants with straw and plastic to keep the fruits clean – or grown up supports.

Melons

Melons are grown indoors in cool climates, like indoor cucumbers, but need a warmer temperature. Watering should be restricted when the fruits are ripening to ensure a good flavour. The flowers will need hand-pollinating: use a small, clean paintbrush to transfer the pollen from a male to a female flower (which has a distinct swelling immediately behind the petals), then remove the male flower immediately after. The fruits will need supporting in loose netting bags as they get heavier.

Courgettes and marrows

Courgette, marrow, gourd, squash and pumpkin seeds need to be kept at a temperature of 15°C (59°F) to germinate well. If the seeds are sown out of doors, sow two or three in each position after all danger of frost has passed and cover the seeds with a cloche or a jam jar. When they germinate, thin out to one plant at each position, discarding the weaker seedlings, and allow about 1m (3ft) between plants. Water and feed regularly. Courgettes should be picked regularly to encourage further fruiting.

GROWING GOURDS OVER AN ARCH

Growing gourds over an arch shows off the brightly coloured fruits, which hang down prettily as bunches of grapes and wisteria flowers do. Small ornamental gourds are best because they are not too heavy, come in a variety of patterns, colours and shapes and can be left on the plant for a long time. If space is tight it is possible to grow courgettes in this way, but because they are grown for eating, the display is continually diminished.

The ideal arches for growing gourds over are the painted metal ones that can be bought in garden centres. They are not too expensive and are easy to erect as they are provided with long metal "legs" which are sunk into the ground. Choose ones with cross pieces up the side for the gourd's tendrils to twine round.

The Turk's cap gourd is particularly decorative grown over an arch. As the fruits get larger, they may need supporting.

Gourds grown over a fence are a decorative way of separating the vegetable plot from the rest of the garden.

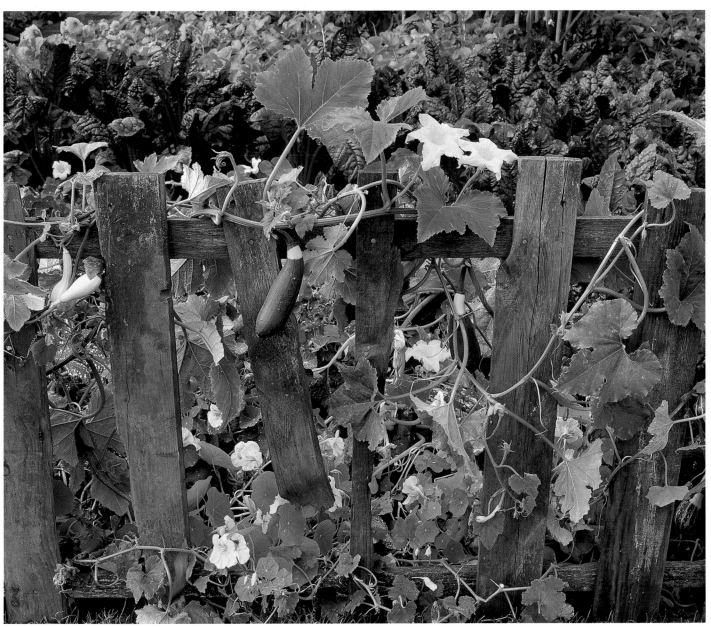

Other produce

THERE ARE OTHER FRUITS PRODUCED on climbing plants like the Chinese gooseberry and passion-fruits that will grow in temperate climates. The plants are vigorous and relatively hardy but need some care to fruit well. At the other extreme are the humble peas and beans which make good, quick screens.

KIWI FRUIT

The Chinese gooseberry or kiwi fruit (*Actinidia deliciosa*) is very vigorous and needs a considerable amount of space. In cool regions it needs to be grown on a warm wall, but where the weather is warmer, it looks magnificent on a well-built pergola. Most actinidia need male and female plants to produce fruit. The late-flowering variety 'Hayward' can be paired with 'Tomari' which flowers at the same time. However, new cultivars have been bred that are self-fertilizing, like 'Jenny' and the much hardier *A. arguta* 'Issai'. This has fragrant flowers and bunches of small fruits.

Training kiwis

After planting, cut the kiwi fruit back to about 30cm (12in) above the ground. Fruiting actinidias are trained like grape vines and need the same system of strong horizontal wires and vertical canes or posts (see pages 70–71).

Tie the stem to the cane and allow side shoots to grow along the horizontal wires. Remove all other shoots. When the horizontal shoots are 1m (3ft) long, stop them. This will encourage the production of lateral shoots. Stop the laterals at five leaves to encourage the growth of fruit-bearing spurs.

In the third summer, the plant should begin fruiting. All fruiting branches should be pinched back to seven leaves after the last fruit. Pinching back laterals without any fruit to five leaves will encourage them to produce fruiting spurs. All extra laterals and sub-laterals should be removed.

KIWIS ON PERGOLAS
In warm regions, kiwi fruits can be attractively trained over a pergola, as they will not need the shelter of a warm wall. The kiwi fruit should be allowed to develop a single main stem up to the top of the pergola, with two leaders trained along the top in opposite directions. The fruiting branches are trained at right angles to the leaders, across the top. The laterals that bear the fruit hang down from the roof.

PASSION-FRUIT

The passion-fruit (*Passiflora edulis*) is the best-known species of the edible passion-flowers. It is not hardy in all areas: it fruits reliably when grown under glass or with a minimum temperature of 10°C (50°F) and with a temperature of at least 16°C (61°F) during the flowering period.

POLLINATION
Under glass and in temperate zones, passion-flowers will need hand-pollinating. Using a clean paintbrush, transfer the pollen from the anthers of one flower to the stigma of another. *P. incarnata*, *P. quadrangularis* and *P. alata* do not readily self-pollinate, so it is necessary to grow two or more plants. The yellow-fruited *P. edulis flavicarpa* can only be cross-pollinated by its purple sibling, *P. edulis*.

How to grow passion-fruit

Passion-fruit can be grown from seed, cuttings or from grafted plants. The plants need supporting on trellis, attached to sturdy uprights sunk into the ground. Prepare the soil by adding well-rotted manure or other organic matter and a high nitrogen fertilizer. Plant the vines about 3–4m (10–12ft) apart. Allow fruiting branches to cascade towards the ground. Keep the plants well-watered and cut back hard after the second year. Add mulch or organic manure every autumn.

Under glass, plants can be grown in containers at least 35cm (14in) across, or in a prepared greenhouse or conservatory bed in well-drained, fertile compost with plenty of organic matter. They will need to be supported on trellis or wires. Train two main stems along wires and pinch out the growing tips when the stems are 60–90cm (24–36in) long. The fruiting laterals will droop towards the ground. Cut back the fruiting stems after they have fruited. Mulch and water as above. Passion-fruits are susceptible to a virus that causes woodiness in the fruit, so plants need to be regularly replaced.

Where space is limited, climbing beans and peas have much to recommend them as they take up little room. They are also attractive enough to grow in ornamental areas, with their large leaves and red, white or lilac flowers and handsome, long pods. They need supporting, first with twiggy sticks, then on canes or pea and bean netting, but they crop well and will provide shelter for more tender crops.

Growing beans

Both climbing French beans and runner beans are available, and can be sown outdoors in their growing positions when any danger of frost has passed and the soil has warmed up. They can also be sown under cloches or in pots on a windowsill or in a greenhouse, earlier in the year.

Sow French beans about 5cm (2in) deep and 20cm (8in) apart. Runner beans are very prolific but need better soil than French beans. Dig the soil deeply and add plenty of

Scarlet runner beans, Phaseolus coccineus, are both decorative and effective grown over arches of bent branches linked with one crosspiece to give stability.

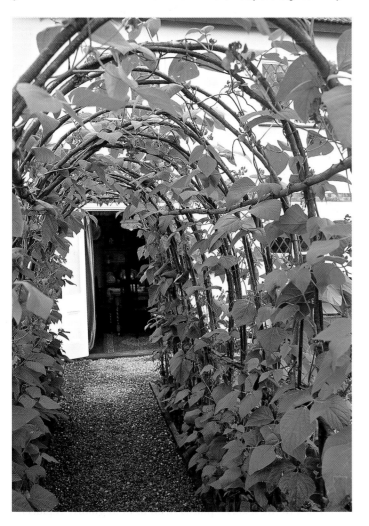

manure the autumn before sowing. Start as for French beans, but sow 5–7.5cm (2–3in) deep, 15cm (6in) apart. When the seedlings are growing, remove every other one, leaving 30cm (12in) between plants.

For continuous flowers, keep picking the beans as soon as they form – unless you are growing some of the decorative beans listed below and want the colour of the pods instead. At the end of the season, leave some of the pods on the plant so that they ripen thoroughly for use as haricot beans.

DECORATIVE BEANS

There are several different colours available which make a very decorative addition to the garden. These plants may not produce as many beans as plain green varieties.
- For **deep purple** beans, try 'Cosse Violette'.
- For **yellow** beans, grow 'Corona d'Oro' or 'Meraviglia di Venesia'.
- For **green with red splashes**, try 'Barlotta Lingua di Fuoco'.
- For **red and white** flowers, you need to grow 'Painted Lady'
- For **white** flowers, try 'Mergoles'.

SUPPORTING BEANS

To make a dense screen of beans, sow two rows, 20cm (8in) apart for French beans or 30cm (12in) apart for runner beans, with the plants staggered. Alternatively, grow the beans up a wigwam of canes. This method is particularly suitable if you are growing the beans in a container.

Growing peas

The taller varieties of peas also make useful screens and are grown in a similar way to beans. Dig plenty of manure or compost into the soil. Sow the seeds 3cm (1in) deep, 5–7cm (2–3in) apart. Main crop peas, like 'Alderman' or 'Show Perfection' grow to about 1.5m (5ft). 'Pilot' another tall variety, is extremely hardy. The 'Carouby de Maussane' is a tall growing mangetout pea which will reach 1.5m (5ft) as does 'Sugar Snap' which can also be eaten pod and all. For something really different try 'Ezetha's Krombek Blauwschok' which has beautiful violet flowers and pods and grows to 1.8m (6ft).

PLANTS FOR WARM PLACES

*T*his chapter looks at some of the tempting climbers that will grow out of doors in warm climates, but need protection and additional heat in cooler regions in the form of a conservatory or greenhouse.

For some climbing plants, humidity as well as high temperatures are required. Many tropical climbers need shade, too: they are native to tropical rainforests and these conditions are difficult to reproduce artificially without a large expenditure of money and effort. Many tropical climbers are also extremely vigorous. In their native habitat they grow to the tops of huge trees, festooning the canopies and flowering out of sight. Choosing the right plants for your conditions is as important in warm climates or a conservatory as it is in cooler ones.

Brilliant bougainvillea looks at its best against Mediterranean blue skies and white painted houses, but it can be grown in a conservatory.

Choosing the right plants

CHOOSING THE RIGHT PLANT is as important in a conservatory or warm climate as it is elsewhere. Wonderful plants like the Jade vine, *Strongylodon macrobotrys*, with long racemes of pea flowers with keels in an exquisite shade of pale green somewhere between jade and aquamarine, unfortunately have to be resisted if you do not own a few acres of rainforest or have a large dedicated glasshouse where this climate type can be replicated. Something less showy that is really happy will be much more satisfying.

CLIMATE ZONES

All of the plants listed in the Plant Directory (see pages 88–93) are given climate zones, which indicate the temperature range they will thrive in.

CLIMATE ZONE	Average Minimum Temperature
ZONE 1	-45.5°C (-50°F)
ZONE 2	-45.5 to -40.1°C (-50 to -40°F)
ZONE 3	-40 to -34.5°C (-40 to -30°F)
ZONE 4	-34.4 to -28.8°C (-30 to -20°F)
ZONE 5	-28.7 to -23.4°C (-20 to -10°F)
ZONE 6	-23.3 to -17.8°C (-10 to 0°F)
ZONE 7	-17.7 to -12.3°C (0 to 10°F)
ZONE 8	-12.2 to -6.7°C (10 to 20°F)
ZONE 9	-6.6 to -1.2°C (20 to 30°F)
ZONE 10	-1.1 to 4.4°C (30 to 40°F)
ZONE 11	4.4°C (over 40°F)

WARM SPOTS OUTSIDE

There are many wonderful, exotic climbing plants that will cope with a slight chill now and then. These are climbers that originate from the Mediterranean, from parts of Australia, California and south America. In northern temperate regions, plants described as hardy in zone 9 may well survive in sheltered town gardens or if grown against south-facing walls. *Araujia sericofera, Clematis armandii, C. cirrhosa* var. *balearica, C. texensis, Eccremocarpus scaber, Passiflora antioquiensis, Solanum jasminoides* 'Album', *Sollya heterophylla,* and *trachelospermums* are all on the borders of hardiness.

WINTER PROTECTION

In a really cold spell, the roots of tender plants can be protected with a thick mulch: a mixture of straw, bracken, dead leaves and woodshavings will suffice.

Evergreen plants are more likely to be killed by frost than deciduous climbers. The well-ripened framework of a

Evergreen *Clematis armandii* flowers in early spring. It is one of the more tender clematis and needs the protection of a warm wall to flower so luxuriantly.

woody climber like *Campsis radicans* can withstand a surprising amount of frost. You can help the ripening process, particularly if the summer has not been a good one, by using high potash fertilizer, like a tomato feed. Follow the manufacturer's instructions.

Plants in pots should be kept very dry during the winter as this helps them to survive the cold.

Climbers against walls can be protected by covering them with horticultural fleece, polythene bubble wrap or a "lean to" of wire netting stuffed with straw or hurdles of reeds propped up against the wall.

HOT DRY CONDITIONS

Hot dry spots either out of doors or in south-facing, sun-baked conservatories make good homes for Greek Island compositions of vivid geraniums and intense bougainvilleas.

CREATING A JUNGLE EFFECT-CONSERVATORY

Most of the large-leaved evergreen climbers need heat and humidity. The large glossy leaves of *Philodendron scandens*, *Syngonium podophyllum*, *Dioscorea discolor*, *Epipremnum aureum* and *Monstera deliciosa* (the Swiss cheese plant) will all give a tropical rainforest effect to a heated but shady conservatory. These plants will thrive indoors because they do not need high light levels and, indeed, are often to be found sold as houseplants. *Aristolochia elegans* with its huge, slightly sinister, maroon and white marbled flowers would also do well in these conditions and create a splendidly exotic effect.

Tropical plants like allamanda, lagenaria, luffa, manettia, nepenthes, granadilla and jade vine all require warm, humid conditions all year round and good light.

Bougainvillea comes in a range of colours, including orange and pink, as well as this pretty rose red. Bougainvillea revels in full sun and a warm climate.

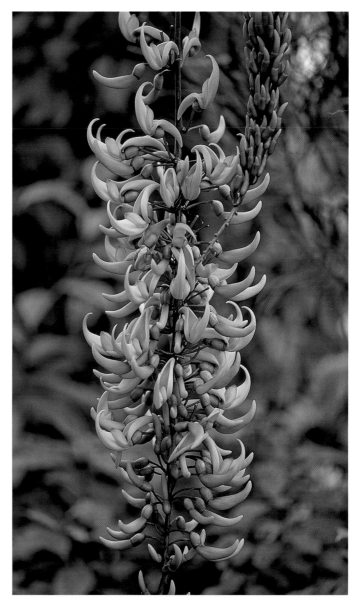

The jade vine, *Strongylodon macrobotrys*, is a fast-growing, twining climber which produces blue-green flowers in long, pendent spikes.

Tropical and sub-tropical conditions

SOME OF THE MOST FLAMBOYANT and exciting climbers need really high temperatures in order to flourish. Others need humidity too. It is important to choose the right plant for your conditions.

TROPICAL PLANTS

A conservatory or glasshouse needs to be kept at a minimum temperature of 16°C (60°F) and over to successfully grow tropical climbers. Below are some examples of plants that will flourish in warm temperatures:

Allamanda cathartica

Antigonon leptopus

Aristolochia elegans

A. gigantea

Bauhinia galpinii

Beaumontia grandiflora

Epipremnum aureum

Clytostoma callistegioides

Hoya bella

Ipomoea alba

Jasminum sambac

Mandevilla × amoena
'Alice du Pont'

Mucuna bennettii

Passiflora alata

P. coccinea

P. racemosa

Petrea volubilis

Senecio macroglossus

Solandra maxima

Solanum wendlandii

Stephanotis floribunda

Stigmaphyllon ciliatum

Strongylodon macrobotrys

Thunbergia grandiflora

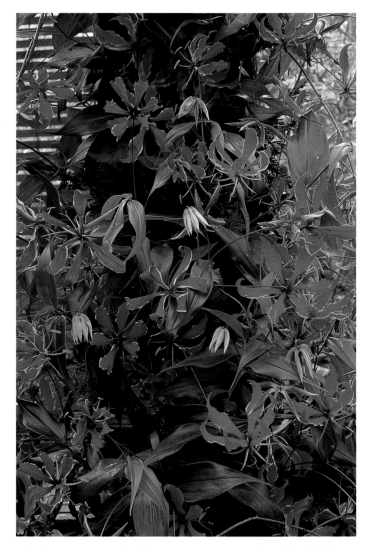

Gloriosa rothschildiana grows from a tuber each spring and dies back in autumn. In warm climates it can be planted in the summer but in temperate zones, pot culture is best.

SUB-TROPICAL PLANTS

Sub-tropical plants need a minimum temperature of 10°C (50°F). The following list suggests a range of plants that can be grown in sub-tropical conditions:

Araujia sericifera

Bomarea caldasii

Bougainvillea spectabilis and
cvs

Chorizema ilicifolium

Cissus antarctica

C. rhombifolia

Distictis buccinatoria

Gelsemium sempervirens

Gloriosa superba

Hardenbergia violacea

Hibbertia scandens

Hoya carnosa

Ipomoea indica

I. purpurea

I. batatas

Kennedia sp.

Lonicera hildebrandiana

Macfadyena unguis-cati

Mandevilla laxa

Metrosideros sp.

Milletia megasperma

Mutisia ilicifolia

Pandorea pandorana

P. jasminoides

Passiflora X allardii

P. X belotii

P. X caeruleoracemosa

P. edulis

P. ligularis

P. manicata

P. mollissima

P. quadrangularis

Plumbago auriculata

Pyrostegia venusta

CONSERVATORY PESTS

As soon as you provide a warm place in winter, pests will find it and multiply, safe from their outdoor predators, and subsist on your precious plants. There are few really effective insecticides, so the answer is vigilance. The first few pests can generally be removed by hand. Large infestations are much more difficult to control.

Ants

Ants build nests in pots and damage plant roots. Water the compost and the base of the conservatory walls with a proprietary ant killer or ant–barrier.

Aphids

Greenfly and blackfly weaken plants and distort leaves by sucking their sap. As soon as you see any signs, squash them. There are several derris, pyrethrum or soap–based insecticides on the market which will keep the numbers down. Grow *Tagetes patula* (French marigolds) in pots to attract hoverflies, the larvae of which eat aphids. Keep the house humid and well ventilated.

Mealybug

These insects are covered with a waxy white powder and white filaments. If you want to try biological control, the predator *Cryptolaemus montrouzierican* can be introduced in late spring. Before that, use a soap–based insecticide.

Red Spider Mite

Signs of infestation are grey or yellowish mottling of leaves and very fine webs on the plants. Increase the humidity by spraying the surrounds and the undersides of the leaves with water frequently. Use biological control by introducing *Phytoseiulus persimilis* as soon as the daytime temperature in the conservatory reaches 21°C (70°F).

Scale Insects

Flat, brown or grey, round or oval scales appear on stems and the undersides of leaves. Like aphids, these are sap suckers. If there are only a few, these can be removed by scraping them off with a fingernail. Currently there are no chemical products on the market that deal with this problem.

Vine Weevil

The larvae of vine weevils eat the roots of plants below the soil. Plants grow very slowly, then wilt and die. Biological control is available: nematodes are watered in to the pots as soon as the compost temperature goes above 12°C (54°F). Vine weevil killers based on imidacloprid are now available and effective. You can also try shaking the plants in the evening and squashing any weevils that fall out.

Whitefly

Whiteflies cover leaves with a sticky honeydew and fly up in clouds from the plants when they are moved. Biological control, the parasitic wasp *Encarsia formosa*, is widely available but the temperature in the conservatory needs to have reached a minimum 10°C (50°F). Before that, use sticky yellow traps or spray with soap–based insecticide or pyrethrum.

Woodlice

These will eat roots and seedlings but mainly live on decaying material. Keep the conservatory clear of dead leaves and plants.

Hanging baskets and containers

HANGING BASKETS AND CONTAINERS are wonderful ways of adding splashes of colour to a garden. Most of the plants used are tender annuals, like petunias and geraniums, but tender climbers are good alternatives and with care, will last from season to season.

Planting a hanging basket

Some smaller tender climbers look very effective in hanging baskets. The long, arching or trailing stems look very graceful cascading down. The baskets can be moved around – in the warmest months they can hang outside in a sheltered sunny spot and as the nights draw in and temperatures start to drop, they can be brought into a sunny conservatory or covered porch.

1 Select the largest hanging basket you can find. The larger they are the easier they are to maintain. Line the basket with moss, bark or fibre.

2 Then line the basket with plastic sheeting which will prevent the compost from drying out too quickly. Make drainage holes in the plastic sheeting (A).

3 Fill the container with good potting compost mixed with added slow release fertilizer granules and a teaspoon or so of water-retaining gel granules.

4 Before planting, water the climbing plants you are going to use in the basket and leave for 30 minutes. Plant into the basket, firming well and watering again (B).

5 Mulch the surface with bark or lightweight aggregate to retain moisture.

A

B

CARING FOR THE BASKET

Hanging baskets are essentially for short-lived display. However, keeping the basket above 10ºC (50ºF) and on the dry side in winter will help the plants. Judicious cutting back in winter is a good idea and the basket should be replanted with fresh compost and slow release fertilizer in spring. Prune again in spring, to strong outward facing buds, to keep the plant in check. The baskets may need watering twice a day in the hottest season.

TENDER CLIMBERS FOR HANGING BASKETS

Bougainvillea glabra 'Harrissii'	*C. rhombifolia*
B. x buttiana 'Rainbow Gold'	*Gelsemium sempervirens*
Chorizema	*Hoya lanceolata bella*
Cissus antarctica	*Maurandya barclaiana*
C. striata	*Pelargonium peltatum*
	Senecio macroglossus
	Thunbergia alata

Planting a Container

Many tropical or sub-tropical plants will grow happily in containers and can thus be grown in cooler regions, as the containers can be moved indoors in the coldest periods of the year. Deciduous or herbaceous plants can be stored in a cellar or garage but must be brought into the light as soon as the weather warms up.

1 Put a drainage layer of crocks, bricks or large stones about 10cm (4in) deep at the bottom of the container (A). This can be covered with a sheet of fibreglass insulation material to prevent fine soil particles washing through and impeding drainage.

2 Fill the container with John Innes No. 3 potting compost mixed with one fifth volume of sand and gravel.

3 This is the point at which to add any supports, canes or pieces of trellis for the plants to grow up.

4 As with hanging baskets, water the climbers in their pots before you plant them. Firm them well in, water again and mulch the surface with bark, gravel or large pebbles (B).

A

B

CHOOSING PLANTS

The following plants do well in containers:

Allamanda cathartica

Bomarea caldasii

Bougainvillea 'Los Banos Beauty'

Bougainvillea 'Temple Fire'

Hibbertia scandens

Manettia bicolor

Mandevilla × amoena 'Alice du Pont'

Mandevilla splendens

Sollya heterophylla

Stephanotis floribunda

CONTAINER CARE

Containers need to be watered regularly, particularly in hot weather, when they should be watered twice a day. A liquid feed prepared according to the manufacturer's instructions, and given weekly, is also advantageous for the plants and will help them to flourish. A yearly top dressing, replacing the top 3cm (1in) of compost in the container with fresh compost, is recommended.

PLANT DIRECTORY

CLIMATE ZONES

All of the plants listed in this Plant Directory are given climate zones, which indicates the temperature range they will thrive in.

Climate Zone	Average minimum Temperature
Zone 1	–45.5°C (–50°F)
Zone 2	–45.5 to –40.1°C (–50 to –40°F)
Zone 3	–40 to –34.5°C (–40 to –30°F)
Zone 4	–34.4 to –28.8°C (–30 to –20°F)
Zone 5	–28.8 to –23.4°C (–20 to –10°F)
Zone 6	–23.3 to –17.8°C (–10 to 0°F)
Zone 7	–17.7 to –12.3°C (0 to 10°F)
Zone 8	–12.2 to –6.7°C (10 to 20°F)
Zone 9	–6.6 to –1.2°C (20 to 30°F)
Zone 10	–1.1 to 4.4°C (30 to 40°F)
Zone 11	4.4°C (over 40°F)

A

Aconitum hemsleyanum (Climbing monkshood) has relatively large mauve-blue flowers. Some clones have better colour than others, so buy it in flower if you can (Zone 8).

Actinidia arguta has satiny green leaves and small fragrant flowers and will grow to be a 20-m (65-ft) tall tree (Zone 4). *A. chinensis*, (Chinese gooseberry or kiwi fruit) will grow to 10m (33ft) or more. The stems and leaves are covered with noticeable red hairs. The heart-shaped leaves can be 15–20cm (6–8in) long. The white flowers are followed by large oval fruits. *A. kolomikta* has long leaves, the upper sections often creamy-white and pink. *A. melanandra* has lance-shaped leaves on long pink stalks and white flowers, followed by egg-shaped fruits (Zone 5).

Adlumia fungosa (Climbing fumitory) has fern-like leaves and drooping pinky-white flowers similar to those of a dicentra (Zone 8).

Akebia quinata (Chocolate vine) is a vigorous twiner with maroon-purple scented flowers in spring and pretty, five-leafleted leaves (Zone 4). *A. trifoliata* has three-lobed leaves, small flowers and larger fruits. *A. × pentaphylla* is a hybrid between them.

Allamanda cathartica (Golden Trumpet) is a scrambling shrub which bears its rich yellow flowers in clusters in summer and autumn. Full sun and plenty of warmth but wind tolerant (Zone 10).

Ampelopsis glandulosa brevipedunculata is a vigorous deciduous tendril climber with lobed dark green leaves and bright blue berries (Zone 4). *A.g.b.* 'Elegans' has pink and white variegated leaves but is frost tender and less vigorous. *A. megalophylla* has the longest leaves of all hardy plants and black berries (Zone 6).

Anredera cordifolia (Mignonette Vine) has highly scented tiny white flowers in racemes in autumn (Zone 9).

Apios americana (Potato bean) is a slender climber with pinnate leaves that flowers in late summer/early autumn, with clusters of pea-shaped flowers in a deep brown-red (Zone 3).

Araujia sericifera (Cruel Plant) traps moths with its sticky pollen at night. It has star-shaped white flowers from late spring to late autumn (Zone 9).

Aristolochia macrophylla (Dutchman's Pipe) is a twining plant with yellowish-green bent tubular flowers with a purple-brown border, but these are often hidden by the heart-shaped leaves which get larger as they age (Zone 4).

Asteranthera ovata has small crinkled leaves and large red trumpet flowers from summer onwards (Zones 8–9).

B

Beaumontia grandiflora (Easter lily vine) has scented white bell-shaped flowers, 12.5cm (5in) long, born in profusion, displayed against large, glossy dark green leaves (Zone 9).

Berberidopsis corallina (Coral plant) has rich, evergreen leaves and hanging clusters of crimson, globular flowers (Zones 8–9).

Billardiera longiflora (Apple Berry) is a slender climber with narrow leaves, greenish-yellow bells, followed by blue berries (Zones 8–9).

Bomarea caldasii has hanging tubular flowers, like an alstromeria, in clusters, that vary from yellow to orange and red (Zones 8–9).

Bougainvillea glabra has woody stems with thorns and brilliantly coloured bracts of cyclamen purple surrounding small white flowers (Zone 9). Most of the cultivars available are *B.g.* crosses, *B. × buttiana* or varieties of *B. spectabilis* and the bracts vary in colour. There are white, orange, scarlet, puce and deep red.

C

Campsis grandiflora has ash-like pinnate leaves and showy orange trumpet flowers with red veins (Zone 7). *C. radicans* has orange tubed, red-petalled flowers and is more vigorous (Zone 4); while *C. × tagliabuana* 'Madame Galen' has salmon-red trumpets, freely borne (Zone 4).

Celastrus orbiculatus (Oriental bittersweet, Staff vine) is an untidy twining plant with rounded leaves but colourful in autumn with red seeds in yellow-lined seed cases and good yellow leaf colour (Zone 4). *C. scandens* (American bittersweet) is less vigorous (Zone 2).

Chorizema cordatum (Australian flame pea) is a perennial climber with bunches of small pea flowers in orange, with a purple keel (Zones 8–9). *C. ilicifolium* (Holly flame pea) has small, holly-like leaves and pink and orange flowers (Zones 8–9).

Cissus antarctica (Kangaroo vine) is a foliage climber, with rich green oval, toothed leaves (Zones 9–10). *C. rhombifolia* (Grape ivy) is similar but with trifoliate leaves (Zones 9–10).

Clematis:
Clematis species and cultivars are hardy, slender plants that climb by using their leaf stalk tendrils. The flowers are

usually made up of four petal-like sepals, which sometimes form a bell shape but are often flat like a saucer.
C. aethusifolia has ferny leaves and pale yellow bell flowers on a delicate plant (Zone 4).
C. alpina has pendulous, lantern-shaped flowers in blue, white or pink in late spring (Zone 5). 'Francis Rivis' is deep blue. 'Ruby' is red. 'Helsingborg' is deep purple.
C. armandii is evergreen with white scented flowers in spring (Zone 7).
C. cirrhosa will climb to 4m (12ft), flowering in winter with creamy-white bells (Zone 7). *C.c. balearica* 'Freckles' has red spots inside.
C. flammula has wiry stems and long panicles of scented white flowers in late summer and autumn (Zone 6).
C. florida 'Sieboldii'has white flowers with a centre of deep purple petaloid stamens (Zone 6).
C. indivisa is evergreen, with glossy leaves and large white flowers (Zone 8).
C. macropetala (Zone 5) As the name indicates, the bell-shaped blue, pink or white flowers on these species are semi-double, the centres full of small, narrow petals. 'Markhams Pink' has mauve-pink flowers. 'Maidwell Hall' is deep blue. Spring flowering.
C. montana (Zone 5) White or pink four-petalled flowers smother this very vigorous plant in late spring/early summer every year. *C.m. grandiflora* has large white flowers. *C.m. var. rubens* has pink flowers. *C.m. var. r.* 'Tetrarose' has larger pink flowers. *C.m. var. r.* 'Freda' has deep cherry-pink flowers and bronze foliage.
C. orientalis has pretty yellow, thick-petalled flowers, followed by fluffy seedheads in late summer and autumn (Zone 6). *C. o.* 'Bill Mackenzie' has larger flowers.
C. rehderiana has cowslip scented small bell flowers of primrose yellow in late summer (Zone 6).
C. terniflora has star-like white flowers in profusion from late summer to mid-autumn.
C. × cartmanii 'Moonbeam' grows to only 1m (3ft) and has greenish-cream flowers in late spring/early summer.
C. × triternata 'Rubromarginata' has clusters of strongly scented white flowers with deep pink margins from mid-summer to early autumn (Zone 5).
Clematis × vedrariensis 'Rosea' is similar to *C.m. var. rubens* except that it has hairs

on the leaves. The variety 'Hidcote' has small, deeper pink flowers.

Viticellas and their hybrids and cultivars are small, late flowering clematis (Zone 4):
'Etoile Violette' – violet.
'Kermesina' – deep red, prolific.
'Madame Julia Correvon' – wine-red with yellow anthers.
'Minuet' – white with reddish-mauve edges.
'Purpurea Plena Elegans'– purple, double flowers.
'Venosa Violacea' – white with violet edges.

Large-flowered hybrids:
'Barbara Jackman' – mauve with a petunia red bar.
'Beauty of Worcester' – violet blue.
'Belle of Woking' – double, silver-mauve.
'Daniel Deronda' – large, deep violet blue, semi-double and single flowers.
'Dr Ruppel' – deep rose pink with a deeper bar.
'Duchess of Edinburgh' – white double flowers.
'Ernest Markham' – purple-red.
'Gravetye Beauty' – deep, rich red, pitcher-shaped flowers.
'Hagley Hybrid'– shell pink.
'Huldine' – white petals with mauve reverse.
'Lasurstern' – very large lavender-blue flowers.
'Mme Baron Veillard' – bright lilac pink.
'Marie Boisselot' – pure white, long flowering.
'Nelly Moser' – large flowers, palest mauve with a pink stripe.
'Niobe' – deep red, free flowering for a long season.
'Perle d'Azur' – the truest blue.
'Scartho Gem' – bright pink with a deeper bar.
'Sylvia Denney' – white with yellow stamens.
'The President' – purple blue, free flowering and compact.
'The Princess of Wales' – bright pink hanging, tulip-shaped flowers.
'Ville de Lyon' – bright crimson red.
'William Kennett' – mid-blue.

Clianthus puniceus (Parrot's beak or Lobster claw) has brilliant scarlet flowers (or you can get coral-pink or white) are borne in clusters of between 6 and 15 blooms each up to 7.5cm (3in) long and attractive foliage (Zone 8).

Cobaea scandens (Cup and saucer vine) is a fast growing perennial with purple bell flowers; there is also a pale green form, sold as 'Alba'. It climbs by leaf tendrils and will flower the first year from seed so can be used as an annual (Zone 9).

Codonopsis convolvulacea is a slender climber that may reach 2m (6ft) with open clusters of lilac-blue bell flowers in late summer (Zone 8).

D

Decumaria barbara is a climbing hydrangea, deciduous or semi-evergreen with clusters of white scented flowers, but without the showy bracts of other climbing hydrangeas (Zone 7). *D. sinensis* is evergreen but less tolerant of cold (Zone 8).

Dicentra scandens (Zone 5) has racemes of pendent yellow, slightly heart-shaped flowers, tipped with pink or light purple and light, ferny foliage. *D. macrocapnos* has similar flowers but is more vigorous.

Dichelostemma volubile is a half-hardy perennial twiner with long allium-like leaves and 1m (3ft) flowering stems with pink flowers (Zone 8).

Distictis buccinatoria (Mexican Blood Flower) has deep rose-crimson tubular flowers, orange-yellow inside and handsome, glossy dark green leaves. It climbs by tendrils which have clinging discs (Zone 9).

E

Eccremocarpus scaber (Chilean glory flower) has orange-red tubular flowers and climbs using many tiny tendrils (Zones 8-9). *E.s. carmineus* is red, *E.s. aureus*, yellow and *E.s. roseus*, pink.

Ercilla volubilis is an evergreen root climber with deep green leaves with paler veins and spikes of whitish pink flowers in spring (Zones 8-9).

Euonymus fortunei is a scandent shrub with handsome, glossy, evergreen leaves (Zone 5). *E. fortunei* 'Silver Queen' has white variegations, *E.f.* 'Emerald 'n' Gold' has bright yellow variegation.
E.f. var. radicans is a particularly good climbing variety, but all climb in the right situation.

F

Fallopia baldschuanica (Russian vine or 'Mile-a-minute') is a deciduous twiner with oval leaves and panicles of small white flowers in later summer (Zone 4).

× *Fatshedera lizei* (Tree ivy) is a scrambling shrub, a cross between ivy and fatsia which has large deeply lobed glossy evergreen leaves (Zone 7).

G

Gloriosa superba (Glory Lily) grows from a tuber and produces slender stems and leaves with long points that taper into a tendril and yellow, ageing to red Turk's cap, lily shaped flowers. *G. rothschildiana* is similar (Zone 9).

H

Hardenbergia violacea (Zone 9), the Vine Lilac or False Sarsparilla, has violet blue pea flowers in long racemes. It will climb to 2m (6ft) and cultivars are available in white and pink as well as violet.

Hedera canariensis 'Ravensholst' is a large-leafed ivy. Leaves can be up to 20cm (8in) long (Zones 7–8).
H. colchica (Persian Ivy) has heart-shaped leaves up to 20cm (8 in) long (Zone 5).
H.c. 'Dentata' has toothed edges.
H.c. 'Dentata Variegata' and *H.c.* 'Sulphur Heart' ('Paddy's Pride') are variegated forms.
H. helix (Common ivy) is a self-clinging climber with dark green leaves and a variable number of lobes (Zone 5).
H.h. 'Atropurpurea' has pale veins and turns purple in autumn.
H.h. 'Chrysophylla' has green and yellow leaves on the same plant. *H.h.* 'Glymii' leaves turn purple in cold.
H.h. 'Goldchild', yellow variegations.
H.h. 'Green Ripple' has deeply cut leaves.
H.h. 'Ivalace' has small dark wavy leaves.
H.h. 'Lemon Swirl', white variegations.
H.h. 'Little Diamond' white variegations.
H.h. 'Oro di Bogliasco', ('Goldheart'), yellow centres.
H.h. 'Parsley Crested' ivy has crimped margins.
H.h. 'Pink and Curly' has crinkled edges with pink on the back.
H.h. 'Sagittifolia', arrow-shaped leaves.
H.h. var. *baltica* is exceptionally hardy.
H. hibernica (Irish ivy) has broad leaves and is a strong grower.
H.h. 'Digitata' has 5 or 7 narrow lobes.

Hibbertia scandens (Gold guinea plant or Snake vine) is a near hardy, twining evergreen with wonderful rich yellow flowers, 5cm (2in) across (Zone 9).

Holboellia coriacea has thick shiny leaves and purple-green male and larger greenish-white female flowers on the plant at the same time in late spring (Zone 7). *H. latifolia* is vigorous with white flowers flushed with purple in late spring (Zone 8).

Humulus lupulus 'Aureus' (Zone 6), the Golden Hop, is a herbaceous twiner with toothed yellowish leaves with three or five lobes.

Hydrangea anomala subsp. *petiolaris*, (Climbing Hydrangea) has small white flowers surrounded by whitish bracts in broad corymbs in midsummer (Zone 4). *H. seemannii* is evergreen, with dark leathery leaves and white flowers (Zone 8).

I

Ipomoeas (Bindweeds or Convolvulus) are fast-growing, twining plants. Some of them can become weeds (Zone 9). *I. alba* (Moonflower) is a herbaceous climber with white trumpets 12.5cm (5in) long (Zones 9–10). *I. batatas* 'Blackie' has deep red leaves and stems, with light purple trumpet flowers (Zone 9). *I. coccinea* is red (Zone 5). *I. indica* is a rich purple. *I. lobata* (sometimes found in catalogues as *Mina lobata*) has small racemes of scarlet flowers fading to white. Seeds are available of 'Flying Saucers', blue and white, or 'Scarlet O'Hara', red. *I. purpurea* has many cultivars in white, pink and scarlet (Zone 5). *I. quamoclit* has small red flowers and feathery leaves. *I.* 'Heavenly Blue' (Morning glory) has large sky-blue flowers (Zone 5).

J

Jasminum azoricum is a semi-twining evergreen with fragrant white flowers, purple in bud (Zone 9). *J. beesianum* has small red flowers with rolled petals (Zone 6). *J. nudiflorum* (Winter jasmine) is a scrambler with yellow flowers in winter (Zone 5). *J. officinale* (Common jasmine) is vigorous with white flowers and is very fragrant (Zones 7–8). *J. polyanthum* has profuse pink flowers and is even more fragrant than the above (Zone 9). *J. sambac* (Arabian jasmine) has very fragrant waxy white jasmine flowers and attractive evergreen foliage (Zone 10). *J.* × *stephanense* is similar to *J. officinale* but with light pink flowers (Zones 7–8).

K

Kadsura japonica is a twining evergreen with creamy yellow flowers from leaf axils between mid-summer and autumn, followed by red fruits (Zone 8).

Kennedia coccinea (Coral pea) has umbels of between three and twelve scarlet pea flowers (Zone 9). *K. nigricans* (Black coral pea) has flowers of yellow and dark browny purple (Zone 9). *K. rubicunda* (Dusky coral pea) has coral-red flowers in small trusses (Zone 9).

L

Lapageria rosea (Chilean bellflower) is a twining evergreen with magnificent large waxy textured bell-shaped flowers in white or pink (Zones 8–9).

Lardizabala biternata is an evergreen twiner with glossy compound leaves and male and female chocolate-purple flowers, followed by purple fruits (Zone 9).

Lathyrus chloranthus has acid yellow pea flowers (Zone 7). *L. grandiflorus* (Everlasting pea) has red and pinky-purple flowers (Zone 6). *L. latifolius* (Perennial sweet pea) has pinky-purple flowers (Zone 5). *L.l.* 'Albus' has white flowers and *L.l.* 'Rosa Perle' is pink. *L. nervosus* 'Lord Anson's Blue Pea' is small with light blue flowers (Zone 7). *L. odoratus* (Sweet pea) in colours from white, pale yellow, mauve, pink, purple and red (Zone 3).

Lonicera × *brownii* (Zones 6–7) Scarlet Trumpet Honeysuckle, red fragrant flowers and oval blue-green leaves. 'Dropmore Scarlet' has a longer flowering season. *L. etrusca* 'Superba' (Zone 7) has creamy-yellow flowers in late summer. *L.* × *heckrottii* (Zone 5) is a scrambler with clusters of yellow flowers, red in bud. *L. henryi* (Zone 5) flowers in midsummer with terminal clusters of small, yellow flowers flushed with reddish purple. *L. hildebrandiana* (Zone 9) is the largest honeysuckle with slender flowers 12–18 cm (5–7in) long. *L.* × *italica* (Zone 5) Free-flowering with clusters of highly scented yellow flowers

flushed with red-purple in summer.
L. japonica (Zones 6–8) is a fast growing evergreen honeysuckle. 'Aureoreticulata' has green leaves netted with yellow; the flowers are insignificant. *L.j.* 'Halliana' and *L.j.* 'Hall's Prolific' have bright green leaves and yellow highly scented flowers. *L. periclymenum* (Zone 4), the Common Honeysuckle or Woodbine, has long tubed flowers, dark purple on the outside and pale pink within. 'Belgica', flowers in mid-summer. 'Graham Thomas' has white flowers ageing to yellow. 'Serotina', or Late Dutch, flowers in late summer. *L. sempervirens sulphurea* (Zone 7), a yellow-flowering form of the Coral Honeysuckle with tubular flowers in drooping spikes and a long flowering period. *L. similis* var. *delavayi*. (Zone 7) Evergreen with large leaves and white strongly scented tubular flowers over a long period. *L. × tellmanniana* (Zone 6) has bright yellow flowers flushed with orange-red. *L. tragophylla* (Zone 6) has large leaves and flowers of bright yellow up to 9cm (3½in) long.

Lophospermum erubescens (Zones 8–9) Perennial twining snapdragons, often called Asarina or even Maurandya, with typical snapdragon flowers in rose pink. Treat as an annual in cool areas. *L. scandens* has lavender flowers.

Lycium chinense (Zone 6) Deciduous scrambler with small purple flowers followed by a profusion of scarlet berries in autumn.

M

Macfadyena unguis-cati (Zones 9–10), the 'Cat's claw vine', is an evergreen tendril climber, grown for its yellow foxglove-like flowers.

Mandevilla laxa (Zone 9), the Chilean jasmine, has highly perfumed white funnel shaped flowers. The foliage is not exciting and it is grown for its perfume. *M. × amoena* 'Alice du Pont' has abundant rose-pink flowers. *M. splendens* (Zones 9–10), large, deep pink flowers.

Maurandella antirrhiniflora (Zones 8–9) is a slender stemmed climber with violet-purple snapdragon flowers. Grow as an annual.

Maurandya barclayana (Zones 8–9) is a woody-based climbing snapdragon

with flowers that vary from white and pink to deep purple.

Menispermum canadense (Zone 4), Moonseed. Woody twiner with circular leaves and blue-black berries in October–November.

Merremia tuberosa (Zone 9), Wood Rose, Yellow Morning Glory. Fast growing evergreen with with funnel-shaped yellow flowers with a deeper coloured throat in summer.

Metrosideros carmineus (Zone 9) A self-clinging evergreen with brilliant scarlet flowers.

Milletia megasperma (Zone 9) The evergreen wisteria has racemes of deep indigo flowers and leathery darker leaves than the deciduous species.

Mitraria coccinea (Zone 8) Evergreen scrambler with scarlet tubular flowers and small dark green leaves.

Mucuna pruriens (Zone 8) The Velvet bean or Florida bean, it has 30cm (12in) racemes of deep purple, or purple black pea flowers.

Muehlenbeckia complexa (Zone 7) Dark purple wiry stems have dark green leaves; tiny star shaped flowers are followed by small white berries.

Mutisia decurrens (Zone 8) has showy bright orange daisy flowers. *M. oligodon* (Zone 8) has orange-pink flowers while those of *M. ilicifolia* (Zone 9) are pink or mauve. It has leathery holly-shaped leaves.

P

Paederia scandens (Zone 7) is a hardy deciduous twiner with dark green leaves and creamy tubular flowers with purple throats. *P. foetida* is lilac; *P. tomentosa*, rose-purple.

Pandorea jasminoides (Zone 9), the Bower of Beauty, has shiny evergreen foliage and foxglove like flowers in pale pink with a red throat. *P. pandorana*, the Wonga-wonga vine, has smaller cream flowers splashed with red or purple.

Parthenocissus henryana (Zone 8), the Chinese Virginia Creeper, has conspicuously white-veined leaves that

turn red in autumn. Insignificant flowers are sometimes followed by blue-black berries.
P. quinquefolia (Zone 3), Virginia Creeper. The leaves made up of five leaflets turn scarlet in autumn.
P. tricuspidata (Zone 4) is often also called the Virginia Creeper. It has maple-like leaves with three lobes. *P. tricuspidata* 'Lowii' has leaves that are cut and crimped at the edges.

Passiflora alata (Zone 9) The flowers are 10–12cm (4–5in) across with dark crimson flowers and hanging filaments striped white and violet.
P. 'Allardii' (Zone 9) has large, scented pink, white and blue flowers.
P. × belotii (Zone 9) Fragrant flowers, 12cm (5in) across in white, pink and blue.
P. caerulea (Zones 8–9), Common or Blue Passion Flower, is almost hardy in the UK. Deeply cut dark green leaves and 6–10cm (2½ to 4in) wide flowers with white sepals and a blue or purple and white banded corona. *P.c.* 'Constance Elliott' (Zones 8–9) is pure white.
P. × caeruleoracemosa (Zone 9) has three-lobed leaves and soft purple flowers.
P. coccinea (Zone 9) has oval leaves and showy scarlet flowers 7–10cm (3–4in) across.
P. edulis (Zone 9), Purple Granadilla, True Passion Fruit, has green and white flowers followed by edible purple fruits.
P. ligularis (Zone 9), the Sweet Granadilla has large white and purple flowers from June to September, followed by sweet, edible fruit.
P. manicata (Zone 9) has large bright scarlet and purple flowers from May to October and edible fruit.
P. mollissima (Zone 9), the Banana Passion Flower, has pink flowers and banana shaped edible fruit.
P. quadrangularis (Zones 9–10), the Giant Granadilla, has large leaves and fragrant bowl-shaped flowers with red petals and purple and white banded filaments.
P. racemosa (Zone 9) has leathery leaves and long, almost leafless sprays of bright red flowers.

Pelargonium peltatum (Zone 9), the Ivy-leaved Geranium, trailing plant with fleshy leaves and, in the species, carmine-red flowers. The cascade pelargoniums like 'Roi de Balcons' derive from this.

Periploca graeca (Zones 7–8), the Common Silk Vine, a deciduous twiner with brownish purple petalled flowers and seeds with silky hairs.

Petrea volubilis (Zones 9–10), the Purple Wreath, has racemes of starry flowers with violet petals and lilac sepals in spring.

Pileostegia viburnoides (Zone 7) is a root climber with long, oval leaves and flattened heads of creamy white flowers in autumn.

Plumbago auriculata (Zone 9), the Cape Leadwort, is a vigorous scrambler with sky–blue flowers a little like primroses.

Pueraria lobata (Zones 7–8), the Kudzu Vine, is a leguminous perennial with trifoliate leaves and racemes of fragrant red–purple pea flowers in late summer.

Pyrostegia venusta (Zone 9–10), the Golden Shower, a vigorous tendril climber with clusters of tubular flowers in a rich golden–orange.

R

Rhodochiton atrosanguineus (Zone 9) is an evergreen perennial which can be grown as an annual. It has long tubular dark purple flowers with a pagoda top in reddish–purple.

Rosa species:
Rosa banksiae (Zones 8–9), the Banksian Rose. *Rb.* 'Lutea' the Yellow Banksian rose is most frequently grown and has violet scented small, double yellow flowers in clusters in spring.
R brunonii (Zone 8), the Himalayan musk rose, has single white flowers in clusters and stems that grow to between 5 and 12 metres long. *Rb.* 'La Mortola' is an even stronger grower.
R canina (Zone 4), the Dog Rose or Common Brier, has single pink flowers and can scramble 5m (15ft) into a tree.
R filipes 'Kiftsgate', (Zone 6) is a robust and extremely vigorous rose with small cream flowers in large trusses, followed by small hips.
R mulligani is less vigorous than *R filipes*, and has single pure white flowers in small clusters.
R setigera (Zone 5), the Prairie Rose, is another scrambler with flowers that vary from crimson to white.
R wichurana (Zones 6–7) has leathery

evergreen leaves and trusses of small white flowers in late summer.

Rosa cultivars:
'Alberic Barbier', a rambler with lustrous foliage and clusters of double, cream flowers.
'Alister Stella Gray', climber with noisette, 7.5 cm (3in) flowers of rich yellow.
'Bobbie James', is a giant rambler with large clusters of creamy white, semi–double flowers.
'Champney's Pink Cluster', a repeat flowering climber with noisette flowers, pink flushed with deeper pink.
'Chewpixel', Open Arms, a miniature rambler with small semi–double pink flowers throughout the summer.
'Chewizz', Warm Welcome, a miniature climber with orange flowers all summer.
'Climbing Cécile Brunner', a vigorous climber with perfect shell pink blooms.
'Climbing Iceberg', medium sized pure white flowers over a long period.
'Crown Princess Margareta', a small climber with neat rosette flowers of apricot–orange.
'Desprez a Fleurs Jaunes', a very old climber with flat, many petalled warm yellow flowers shaded with peachy pink.
'Dr W. Van Fleet', a rambler with soft pink flowers and glossy foliage.
'Easlea's Golden Rambler', is a rich yellow and blooms once.
'Evangeline', a rambler with clusters of soft, pinkish–white flowers late in the season.
'Excelsa', Red Dorothy Perkins, has large trusses of light crimson flowers and very dark green leaves.
'Félicité Perpétue', a rambler with neat foliage and double, creamy white pompom flowers from pink buds.
'Gertrude Jekyll', neat buds expand into large Old Rose shaped rich pink rosettes.
'Guinee', climber with highly scented and darkest crimson flowers of any rose.
'Handel', is a modern climber with cream flowers edged with rose–pink.
'Lawrence Johnson', a strong growing climber with canary yellow flowers once in the season.
'Little Rambler', has small double flowers of light pink that pale as they age. Repeat flowering.
'Madame Alfred Carrière', hardy, noisette–flowered climber with white flowers tinted with soft pink.
'Madame Grégoire Staechelin', Spanish Beauty, large semi–double flowers in

glowing pink, in clusters. Flowers once.
'Maigold', bronze–yellow semi–double flowers, once flowering, early in season.
'Mermaid', large, single canary yellow flowers over the summer.
'Paul's Himalayan Musk', rambler with open sprays of blush–pink rosette flowers in profusion.
'Paul's Scarlet Climber', large clusters of brilliant scarlet flowers.
'Phyllis Bide', a repeat flowering rambler, small yellow flowers flushed with pink.
'Rambling Rector', a strong climber with creamy flowers that open white, showing yellow stamens, followed by red hips.
'Sombreuil', climber, flat quartered flowers of white tinged with flesh–pink.
'Treasure Trove', a vigorous rambler with apricot–pink flowers.
'Veilchenblau', an almost thornless rambler with small semi–double flowers that start purple and age to lilac.
'Wedding Day', a prolific rambler with yellow buds that open to cream and then turn white.
'White Cockade', an upright climber, small glossy leaves and double pure white flowers.
'Zéphirine Drouhin', deep pink roses produced over a long period and in profusion. Thornless.

Rubus flagelliflorus, (Zone 7) graceful scrambler with white–felted stems and shiny black fruits.
R fruticosus laciniatus 'Oregon Thornless', the Thornless blackberry (Zone 4).
R.f.l. 'Parsley Leaved', decorative ferny leaves and good edible black fruits.
R ichangensis (Zone 6) Semi–evergreen heart–shaped leaves, panicles of white flowers and edible fruits. *R irenaeus* has large round leaves, small white flowers followed by large red fruits. *R lineatus* (Zone 8) semi–evergreen with white–veined leaves like a horse chestnut, small fruit and flowers. *R phoenicolasius* (Zone 5), the Japanese wineberry; red bristled stems, light green leaves with white undersides, flowers encased by red–haired sepals, conical red edible fruits. *R ulmifolius* 'Bellidiflorus' (Zone 4), small pink pompom flowers on this blackberry relation.

S

Schisandra chinensis (Zone 5) Woody stemmed twiner with white or pale pink flowers borne in clusters in late spring. *S. rubriflora* (Zone 8) has small crimson flowers and red fruits. *S. sphenanthera* (Zone 7) has terracotta coloured flowers in early summer.

Schizophragma hydrangeoides (Zone 5) is a self-clinging hydrangea with dark heart shaped leaves and cream flowers in lacy clusters surrounded by elegant bracts. *S. integrifolium* (Zone 7) is similar but has larger flower heads.

Senecio macroglossus (Zone 9), Cape Ivy or Wax Vine. Thick glossy leaves and white daisy flowers. *S.m.* 'Variegatus' has yellow variegations.

Smilax aspera (Zone 7), Rough Bindweed, thorny herbaceous perennial climber with pale, glossy leaves, small scented flowers and glossy red berries later. *S. rotundifolia* (Zone 4), Horse brier, glossy heart shaped leaves, yellow green flowers in summer followed by black berries covered with a white patina.

Solanum crispum 'Glasnevin' (Zone 8) Blue–purple potato flowers on a scrambling semi–woody shrub. Long flowering, semi–evergreen. *S. dulcamara* 'Variegatum' (Zone 4), Variegated Woody Nightshade. Trailing perennial with poisonous red berries. *S. jasminoides* 'Album' (Zones 8–9), Potato vine, is a true climber with twining leaf stalks. Pure white potato flowers from July to autumn. *S. wendlandii* (Zone 9), Giant Costa Rican Potato Vine, evergreen, climbs using sharp hooks. Lavender blue flowers, 6cm (2½in) across in large bunches.

Sollya heterophylla (Zone 9), the Australian bluebell, is a perennial with pale green lanceolate leaves and sky–blue bell–shaped flowers, 1cm (½in) long.

Stauntonia hexaphylla, with dark glossy leaves and small clusters of white, fragrant flowers in spring, is another example of a very slightly tender plant which is well worth trying. In a good year, it even produces purple–red fruits.

Stephanotis floribunda, (Zone 10), the Wax Flower, a twining plant which has waxy pure white flowers and shiny evergreen leaves.

T

Teucrium fruticans (Zone 9) a scrambling shrub with oval grey–green leaves and small lipped blue flowers on white stems, June to September.

Thladiantha dubia (Zone 8), a herbaceous perennial, growing to 5m (15ft). Heart shaped leaves and bright yellow bell–shaped flowers. It is a member of the cucumber family.

Thunbergia alata (Zone 5), Black–Eyed Susan. Annual twiner with 5cm (2in) wide flowers with chocolate brown centres. Colours range from white through yellow to orange. *T. grandiflora*, (Zones 9–10, or Zone 6 as an annual), the Blue trumpet vine, Blue Skyflower, a vigorous woody–stemmed climber with large blue flowers. *T. gregorii* (Zone 9, Zone 5 as an annual) has 5cm (2in) wide flowers of bright orange. *T. mysorensis* (Zones 9–10) has long racemes of golden flowers with brownish–red to purple tubes.

Trachelospermum asiaticum (Zone 9), the Star Jasmine, has glossy dark green leaves in opposite pairs and small clusters of jasmine–like scented white flowers. *T. jasminoides* (Zone 9) is a taller, better plant but needs more support and is less hardy. The leaves of *T.j.* 'Variegatum' have white edges.

Tripterygium regelii (Zone 4) grows to about 6m (18 feet). It has handsome oval leaves about 15cm (6in) long. In late summer, panicles of small white flowers are followed by greenish fruits with three wings.

Tropaeolum azureum (Zone 9) is a slender trailer with blue flowers shaped like a mimulus, slenderly lobed leaves. *T. majus* (Zone 5) is the annual nasturtium available as seed in yellows, oranges, reds. *T. peregrinum* (Zone 5), the Canary Creeper, grows to about 1.5m (5ft) and has small yellow fringed flowers. *T. speciosum* (Zone 8), the Flame Vine, has vivid red flowers followed by deep blue fruits contrasting with purplish bracts. *T. tricolorum* (Zones 8–9) which grows to about 120cm (4ft) has striking orange or yellow flowers from red–orange black–tipped calyces. *T. tuberosum* (Zone 8, but the tubers can be replanted annually) of which the most widely available form is *T. tuberosum* var. *lineamaculatum* 'Ken Aslet' which has blue–green leaves and long spurred orange red flowers.

Tweedia caerulea (Zone 9) A small perennial twiner to about 1m (3ft) with narrow oblong grey leaves and clusters of turquoise–blue flowers.

V

Vinca major (Zone 7), the Greater Periwinkle, has shiny, rich green leaves and blue flowers. It will scramble through a shrub.

Vitis amurensis (Zone 4) is similar to the grape vine and has broad leaves which colour to red and purple in the autumn. *V.* 'Brant' (Zone 4) has leaves which turn bronze–red and purple in autumn. *V. coignetiae* (Zone 5) will grow to 20m (60ft) and has large 15–30 cm (6–12in) leaves which turn scarlet and apricot in autumn. *V. davidii* (Zone 6) has bristly stems and heart–shaped leaves which turn crimson in autumn. The small black grapes are edible. *V. labrusca* 'Concord' (Zone 5), the Fox Grape. It has thick textured leaves and very good fruit. *V. parvifolia* (Zone 5) syn. *V. flexuosa*, has small bronze–green shiny leaves, fluffy flowers and good autumn colour. *V. riparia* (Zone 2), the Riverbank Grape, has heart–shaped leaves and exceptional autumn colour. *V. thunbergii* (Zone 6) is less vigorous; the leaves are brown–felted underneath and turn scarlet in autumn. *V. vinifera* (Zone 6), the Grape Vine, is deciduous. *V.v.* 'Ciotat' has finely dissected leaves. *V.v.* 'Purpurea' has claret red leaves when young which turn to red–purple as they age.

W

Wisteria:
Wisterias are vigorous woody twining plants with pinnate ash–like leaves and showy pendent racemes of pea flowers, varying in length from 10cm (4in) to 1m (3¼ft).
Wisteria brachybotrys (syn.*W. venusta*) (Zone 5) has chunky racemes of white flowers about 10–15cm (4–6in) long. *W. floribunda* 'Alba' (Zone 4), the Japanese wisteria, has racemes of white flowers that can be over a metre in length. *W.f.* 'Multijuga' has lilac blue flowers. *W. sinensis* (Zone 5), the Chinese wisteria, has shorter racemes of mauve to deep lilac flowers, between 12 and 25cm (5 to 10in) long. *W.s.* 'Prolific' is very vigorous.

Suppliers

UK

Caddick's Clematis Nursery
Lymm Road
Thelwall, Warrington
Cheshire WA4 2TG
Tel: (01925) 757196
www.caddicks-clematis.co.uk
Clematis

Cranborne Manor Nursery
Cranborne, Wimborne
Dorset BH21 5PP
Tel: (01725) 517248
www.cranborne.co.uk
*Old fashioned climbing and rambling roses,
large selection of clematis*

David Austin Roses
Bowling Green Lane
Albrighton
Wolverhampton WV7 3HB
Tel: (01902) 376300
www.davidaustinroses.com
English roses, climbing and rambling roses

Greenholm Nurseries Ltd
Lampley Road
Kingston Seymour
Clevedon
Avon BS21 9XS
Tel: (01934) 833350
Passionflowers

Ken Muir Ltd
Honeypot Farm
Rectory Road
Weeley Heath
Clacton-On-Sea
Essex CO16 9BJ
Tel: (01255) 830181
www.kenmuir.co.uk
Fruit

Pennells Nurseries
www.pennells.co.uk
*Specialists in clematis – wholesalers,
with outlets at:*
Hykeham Garden Centre
Newark Road, South Hykeham
Lincoln LN6 9NT
Tel: (01522) 880033
&
Grimsby/Cleethorpes Garden Centre
Humberston Road
Cleethorpes DN36 4RW
Tel: (01472) 313600

Peter Beales Roses
London Road
Attleborough
Norfolk NR17 1AY
Tel: (01953) 454707
www.peterbealesroses.com
Roses

Read's Nursery
Hales Hall
Loddon
Norfolk NR14 6QW
Tel: (01508) 548395
www.readsnursery.co.uk
Conservatory plants and fruit

R. Harkness and Co. Ltd
Hitchin
Herts SG4 0JT
Tel: (01462) 420402
www.roses.co.uk
Specialists in roses

Roseland House Garden and Nursery
Chacewater, Truro
Cornwall TR4 8QB
Tel: (01872) 560451
www.roselandhouse.co.uk
Specialize in climbing and conservatory plants

Rumwood Nurseries and Garden Centre
Langley, Maidstone
Kent ME17 3ND
Tel: (01622) 861477
www.rumwoodnurseries.co.uk
Specialize in roses, but do sell other climbing plants

Sherston Parva Nursery Ltd
Malmesbury Road
Sherston
Wiltshire SN16 0NX
Tel: (01666) 841066
Clematis and other climbers

Taylors Nurseries
Sutton Road
Sutton
Askern
Doncaster DN6 9JZ
Tel: (01302) 700716
www.taylorsclematis.co.uk
Clematis

Thorncroft Clematis Nursery
Reymerston, Norwich
Norfolk NR9 4QG
Tel: (01953) 850407
www.thorncroft.co.uk
Clematis

SOUTH AFRICA

Gardenshop
P.O. Box 70966
BRYANSTON 2021
www.gardenshop.co.za
Branches at:
Bryanston
Tel: (011) 463-5773
Fax: (011) 463-5775
&
Fourways
Tel: (011) 465-2226
Fax: (011) 465-2712
&
Parktown North
Tel: (011) 447-2368
Fax: (011) 880-4225

Lifestyle Garden Centre
P.O. Box 2568
NORTHCLIFF 2115
Tel: (011) 792-5616
Fax: (011) 792-5626
www.lifestyle.co.za

Flora Farm
P.O. Box 25730
EAST RAND 1462
Tel: (011) 894-2377
Fax: (011) 894-5482

Safari Garden Centre
P.O. Box 72244
LYNWOOD RIDGE 0040
Tel: (012) 807-0009
Fax: (012) 807-0350

The Jungle Nursery
P.O. Box 30988
MAYVILLE 4058
Tel: (031) 207-7642
Fax: (031) 207-7642

Starke Ayres
21 Liesbeeck Park Way
Rosebank
CAPE TOWN 7700
Tel: (021) 685-4120
Fax: (021) 685-3837
www.thegardencentre.co.za

Stodels Nurseries
P.O. Box 3060
Tygerpark
CAPE TOWN 7536
Tel: (021) 919-1106
Fax: (021) 919-9324

Stodels Nurseries
Doncaster Road
Kenilworth
CAPE TOWN 7700
Tel: (021) 671-9050
Fax: (021) 741507

Super Plants
P.O. Box 212
Table View
CAPE TOWN 7439
Tel: (021) 558-0190
Fax: (021) 558-5413
www.superplants.co.za

AUSTRALIA

NSW
Flower Power Garden Centres
124 Newbridge Rd
MOOREBANK
NSW 2170
Tel: (02) 9601 4555

Simply d'vine Gardens & Gifts
49 Orient St
NULKABA
NSW 2325
Tel: (02) 4990 4291

NT
Alice Springs Nursery
Ross Hwy
NT 0870
Tel: (08) 8952 5055

VIC
Essendon Garden Centre
1060 Mt Alexander Rd
ESSENDON
VIC 3040
Tel: (03) 9379 0555

Gardenworld
810-834 Springvale Rd
KEYSBOROUGH
VIC 3173
Tel: (03) 9798 8095

SA
Heyne's Nurseries Pty Ltd
287 The Parade
BEULAH PARK
SA 5067
Tel: (08) 8332 2933

Thomson David Nursery
Gores Rd
SUMMERTOWN
SA 5141
Tel: (08) 8390 3189

QLD
Aspley Nursery
341 Maundrell Tce
ASPLEY
QLD 4034
Tel: (07) 3263 9444

Brookfield Garden Centre
2371 Moggill Rd
BROOKFIELD
QLD 4069
Tel: (07) 3878 7739

TAS
Plants Plus
15385 Bass Hwy
SOMERSET
TAS 7322
Tel: (03) 6435 1391

Tasman Nursery
1169 Acton Rd
CAMBRIDGE
TAS 7170
Tel: (03) 6248 5040

WA
Cornerstone Garden Centre
794 North Lake Rd
JANDAKOT
WA 6164
Tel: (08) 9417 8512

Sunflower Garden Centre
736 Karrinyup Rd
OSBORNE PARK
WA 6017
Tel: (08) 9349 8883

Recommended Reading

Classic Roses, by Peter Beales, Harvill Press, 1997, ISBN 1 86046 302 9.

The Complete Guide to Pruning and Training Plants, by David Joyce and Christopher Brickell, Simon & Schuster, 1992, ISBN 0 67173 842 9.

Creative Vegetable Gardening, by Joy Larkcom, Mitchell Beazley, 2000, ISBN 1 84000 292 1.

Hamlyn Care Manual: Roses, by Amanda Beales, Hamlyn, 2001, ISBN 0 60060 433 0.

The Royal Horticultural Society Encyclopedia of Gardening, ed. Christopher Brickell, Dorling Kindersley, 1993, ISBN 0 86318 979 2.

The Royal Horticultural Society: Growing Fruit, by Harry Baker, Mitchell Beazley, 1999, ISBN 1 84000 153 4.

The Royal Horticultural Society: Pests & Diseases, by Pippa Greenwood and Andrew Halstead, Dorling Kindersley, 1997, ISBN 0 75130 366 6.

PICTURE CREDITS

Clive Nichols: pages 2 (Dinmor Manor, Worcs.), 8/9 (Rupert Golby), 23 (right) (Dinmor Manor, Worcs.), 24/25, 26, 28, 29 (Elisabeth Woodhouse), 36/37 (Eastleach House, Glos.), 38 (Vale End, Surrey), 45 (Rosendal, Sweden), 46/47 (also on back of jacket) (Eastleach House, Glos.), 50, 54 (Wollerton Old Hall, Shrops.), 55 (detail) (Eastleach House, Glos.), 56, 57 (Meadow Plants, Berks.), 60/61, 67 (bottom) (Eastleach House, Glos.), 73 (The Abbey House), 74, front of jacket (Leightholme Dale Lodge, Yorks.).

Garden Matters: pages 6 (left), 6 (right), 7 (left), 7 (middle), 7 (right), 15, 19, 20, 23 (left), 30, 31, 32, 34, 40, 44, 49, 51, 52, 63, 65, 67 (top) (detail also on jacket spine), 70, 77 (top), 79, 80/81, 83 (left), 84.

Derek St Romaine Photography: pages 58, 62, 68/69, 77 (bottom), 82, 83 (right).

Index